DINNER'S READY

DINNER'S READY

Daphne Metaxas Hartwig

A BOBBS-MERRILL BOOK

MACMILLAN PUBLISHING COMPANY

New York

COLLIER MACMILLAN PUBLISHERS

London

Macmillan Publishing Company
866 Third Avenue, New York, N.Y. 10022
Collier Macmillan Canada, Inc.

Library of Congress Cataloging-in-Publication Data
Hartwig, Daphne Metaxas.
Dinner's ready.
"A Bobbs-Merrill book."
Includes index.
1. Cookery.   I. Title.
TX652.H3718   1987   641.5'55   86-23546
ISBN 0-02-548531-8

Macmillan books are available at special discounts for bulk purchases
for sales promotions, premiums, fund-raising, or educational use.
For details, contact:
Special Sales Director
Macmillan Publishing Company
866 Third Avenue
New York, N.Y. 10022

Illustrations by Thelma Gomilas
Book design by Lynn Fischer

10 9 8 7 6 5 4 3 2 1

Printed in the United States of America

To Glenn "Fat-Boy" Hartwig
and to
Theone, Mom, and Dad

❧ CONTENTS ❧

CONTENTS

➳ INTRODUCTION ᩖ

If hectic, grab-anything dinners have become a way of life at your house, this book can restore a relaxed, satisfying dinnertime to each of your busy family members no matter how conflicting their schedules.

DINNER'S READY consists of specially designed recipes for meals that are preassembled but not-yet-cooked. The meals wait in your refrigerator to be completed at a moment's notice and take from 2 to 20—the average being 10—minutes to cook and serve. With each recipe, you can cook portions individually to accommodate family members who must eat either before or after the rest of the family *and* you can cook multiple servings for those family members who have the time to share a leisurely dinner together. The end result is that everyone in your family can enjoy the same balanced, freshly cooked meal no matter what time their schedules permit while you are spared any frantic, beat-the-clock preparations to meet their needs.

The recipes in this book are easy to prepare and never rely on expensive ingredients to speed up the cooking time. The resulting meals are varied and geared to please a wide range of family taste preferences. Some recipes can easily be used as made-in-advance dinners for entertaining, while others are simple enough for older children and teenagers to prepare for themselves.

Chapters in this book include: preassembled main dishes that cook up in short order; ready-made, single-serving casseroles; no-thaw freezer-to-oven dinners; and marinated meats waiting to be broiled. There are also: ready-made components that assemble instantly; prepared-in-advance stir-fry ingredients; soups and stews that wait on your stovetop; ready-to-eat room-temperature meals; and hot supper sandwiches. The last two chapters include portable, hand-held meals for people in a real hurry and ready-to-eat side dishes served straight from the refrigerator.

So, when there are late work nights, high school basketball games, music lessons, Girl Scout meetings, night classes, or just plain hectic days, you don't have to turn to reheated casseroles, hot dogs, expensive convenience foods, or a fast-food drive-up window. The specially designed recipes from this book will enable every member of your family, including yourself, to enjoy an unhurried, freshly made quality dinner.

❧ 1 ❧

READY-TO-COOK
MAIN DISHES

These completely preassembled main dishes can wait in your refrigerator to be cooked at a moment's notice in either individual or multiple servings.

Chicken Cutlets Dijon

Chicken Cutlets Bolognese

Tender, Crusty Turkey Meatballs

Wine and Cumin Beef Rolls

Lemon-Herbed Meatballs with Buttered Spaghetti

Country-Style Barbecued Ribs

Pork Balls with Ginger-Orange Glaze

Kulebiaka Pastries

Baked Fish Florentine

Fish Kabob Roll-Ups

Seafood Chowder

Chicken Cutlets Dijon

Serves 4 to 6
Cooking Time: 5 minutes

4 to 6 chicken thighs
1 cup all-purpose flour
2 large eggs
6 tablespoons Dijon mustard
1 tablespoon dried parsley
  flakes, crushed between the
  heels of your hands

1 ½ teaspoons salt
¼ teaspoon pepper
2 cups fine dry bread crumbs
3 to 4 tablespoons butter
3 to 4 tablespoons olive oil

Remove the skin and bones from the chicken thighs, cutting the meat of each thigh into 2 pieces. Place each chicken piece between generous doubled lengths of plastic wrap. Pound each piece with a mallet or the bottom of a flat heavy skillet until the meat is thin but not shredded. Set the cutlets aside.

Put ⅓ cup of the flour into a shallow soup bowl for dredging. In a second shallow bowl, beat the eggs until they are bubbly; then blend in the mustard. In a third, larger bowl, blend together the remaining ⅔ cup of flour, the parsley, salt, and pepper; stir in 1¼ cups of the bread crumbs. Sprinkle a large baking sheet with the remaining ¾ cup of bread crumbs; set the baking sheet aside.

Unwrap the first piece of chicken and dip it into the dredging flour on both sides, shaking off any excess flour. Then dip the piece in the egg–mustard mixture to coat it generously on both sides. Then coat the piece thoroughly in the bread crumb mixture and transfer it to the baking sheet. When all the chicken pieces have been coated in this manner, cover the baking sheet with plastic wrap and refrigerate it until dinnertime.

To Cook an Individual Serving

Heat 1 tablespoon of butter and 1 tablespoon of olive oil in a small skillet over medium-high heat. When the butter and oil just begin to bubble, add 2 or 3 coated cutlets and sauté on both sides for about 5 minutes, or until nicely browned and just tender.

To Cook Multiple Servings

Heat 1 tablespoon of butter and 1 tablespoon of oil for every 4 cutlets, using a larger skillet. Cook as directed above.

Chicken Cutlets Bolognese

Serves 4
Cooking Time: 20 minutes

4 chicken thighs or breast
   halves
¼ cup plus 1 tablespoon
   all-purpose flour
⅛ teaspoon pepper
2 tablespoons butter

2 tablespoons olive oil
2 cups loosely-packed
   shredded Monterey Jack
   cheese (about 6 ounces)
8 very thin slices boiled ham

Remove the skin and bones from the chicken pieces. If you are using thighs, cut each thigh into 2 equal pieces as you remove the bone; if using breast halves, slice each in half to get 8 pieces. Place each chicken piece between generous doubled lengths of plastic wrap. Pound each piece with a mallet or the bottom of a flat heavy skillet until the meat is thin but not shredded.

In a shallow bowl, blend ¼ cup of the flour with the pepper. Unwrap 4 of the pounded chicken pieces and dredge them on both sides in the flour; shake off any excess flour.

Heat 1 tablespoon of the butter and 1 tablespoon of the oil in a skillet over medium-high heat. When the butter and oil just begin to bubble, add the 4 floured chicken pieces and sauté for about 4 to 5 minutes, turning the pieces so that both sides become golden brown and just tender; do not be tempted to overcook them. Transfer the cutlets to a 10- by 15-inch baking pan. Repeat the dredging and sautéing of the remaining 4 cutlets, using the rest of the butter and oil as necessary. Let the cutlets cool to room temperature in the baking pan.

Divide the shredded cheese equally between 2 bowls; toss the remaining tablespoon of flour into only one bowl so that the cheese becomes dusted and no longer sticky; leave the other bowl of cheese unfloured. Carefully sprinkle the flour-dusted cheese equally over each chicken cutlet in the baking pan; press the cheese gently onto the cutlets with your hand. Place a slice of ham, folded, if necessary, over the layers of cheese on each cutlet. Carefully sprinkle and gently press the second, unfloured portion of cheese over each slice of ham. Cover the baking pan with plastic wrap and refrigerate until ready to use—for up to 2 days.

To Cook an Individual Serving

Preheat the oven to 350 degrees. Use a spatula to transfer 2 of the prepared cutlets onto an accommodating baking pan. Bake, uncovered, for 20 minutes, or until the cheese is nicely melted.

To Cook Multiple Servings

Cook following the directions above, using 2 prepared cutlets for each serving.

Tender, Crusty Turkey Meatballs

Serves 4
Cooking Time: 5 to 10 minutes

2 cups Croutettes Herb-Seasoned Stuffing Mix cubes, or any other plain or onion-flavored croutons	¾ cup milk
	1 pound ground raw turkey, fresh or frozen and thawed
1½ tablespoons snipped fresh dillweed, or 1½ teaspoons dried dill	2 cups fine dry bread crumbs
	½ cup all-purpose flour
	Oil for frying
	Salt, optional

Combine the stuffing mix, dill, and milk in a large bowl; let soak for 10 minutes. Beat the mixture with a potato masher or a fork until it is mushy; then mix in the ground turkey with your hands; set it aside. Spread ½ cup of the bread crumbs evenly over a 10- by 15-inch or similar baking pan; set it aside.

In a mixing bowl, combine the remaining 1½ cups of bread crumbs with the flour to make a coating mixture. Drop a rounded teaspoon of the meat mixture into the coating mixture; use your hands to gently cover the meat well on all sides, so that you embed the meat with the coating mixture while forming a slightly flattened meatball 1½ to 2 inches wide. Gently set the meatball on the crumbed pan; repeat the procedure until you have used all the meat mixture. When all the meatballs are made, sprinkle a handful of the remaining coating mixture over the pan of meatballs. Cover the pan with plastic wrap and refrigerate until ready to use—for up to 2 days.

To Cook an Individual Serving

Pour oil into a small skillet to a depth of ¼ inch; heat over high heat until a drop of water flicked into the oil sizzles or pops. Sauté one fourth of the meatballs in the oil until they are amber-brown and crusty on one side; lower the heat to medium-high if it becomes necessary. Using tongs to handle them, turn the meatballs over and sauté on the other side until they are amber-brown and crusty. Transfer to a dinner plate and sprinkle lightly with salt, if you wish, before serving.

To Cook Multiple Servings

Use a larger skillet but keep the depth of the oil at ¼ inch. Cook following the directions above, using one fourth of the refrigerated meatballs for each serving. When cooked, transfer the meatballs to a serving dish lined with several layers of paper towels; sprinkle lightly with salt, if you wish, before serving.

Wine and Cumin Beef Rolls

Serves 4
Cooking Time: 10 to 15 minutes

SAUCE

1 6-ounce can tomato paste
2½ tomato paste cans of water
1 tablespoon olive oil
1 teaspoon sugar
½ teaspoon salt, optional
¼ teaspoon pepper

ACCOMPANIMENTS

1 loaf crusty Italian bread
4 individual tossed salads

MEAT ROLLS

4 slices white bread with crusts
    removed
½ cup dry red wine
1 large egg
3 large garlic cloves, smashed
    and very finely minced
1 tablespoon ground cumin
2 pounds ground beef
⅓ cup olive oil for frying

Blend all the sauce ingredients together in a 3-quart pot. Then bring to a boil over medium heat, cover, and simmer over low heat for 5 minutes. Remove the pot from the heat, set the cover ajar, and let the sauce cool while you make the meat rolls.

In a large bowl, soak the white bread in the wine for 5 minutes; then squish the bread into small pieces with your hands. Add the egg, garlic, and cumin; beat them lightly into the soaked bread. Add the meat, tossing and mixing well with your hands. Lightly moisten your hands and roll the mixture into cylinders 2 to 2½ inches long and as thick as a broomstick; taper the ends.

Heat the oil in a heavy skillet over medium-high to high heat. When a drop of water flicked into the oil sizzles, add half of the meat rolls; use tongs to turn the rolls on all sides until they are brown and somewhat solid. Line a 10- by 15-inch or similar baking sheet with paper towels; transfer the cooked meat rolls to this. Cook and transfer the other half of the meat rolls in the same manner. Let the rolls cool to room temperature; then cover the baking sheet with plastic wrap and refrigerate until ready to use—for up to 2 days. Also, cover the cooled sauce in its pot and refrigerate.

Make 4 individual-size tossed salads but do not add any dressing; cover with plastic wrap and refrigerate.

To Cook an Individual Serving

Bring the whole pot of sauce to a gentle boil over medium heat. Drop one fourth of the cooked meat rolls into the sauce and simmer, covered, for 10 to 15 minutes, or until they are heated through.

Use a slotted spoon to transfer the rolls to a shallow soup bowl. Remove the pot of sauce from the heat and, after one dinner, refrigerate for later use by others. Serve with several slices of the crusty bread and one of the salads to which you have added the dressing.

To Cook Multiple Servings

Cook following the directions above, using one fourth of the cooked meat rolls for each serving. You could also warm the crusty bread in a 200-degree oven while the meat rolls simmer.

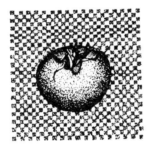

Lemon-Herbed Meatballs with Buttered Spaghetti

Serves 4
Cooking Time: about 15 minutes

1 lemon
3 slices white bread with crusts
  removed
¼ cup water
1 large egg, lightly beaten
¼ cup grated Parmesan cheese
2 tablespoons minced fresh
  parsley, or 2 teaspoons dried
  parsley flakes
3 medium-size garlic cloves,
  smashed and very finely
  minced

Pepper to taste
1 pound ground beef
1 pound Italian sweet sausage
8 tablespoons (1 stick) butter
1 8-ounce box spaghetti
Salt to taste
Grated Parmesan cheese for
  sprinkling
About ½ cup olive oil for
  frying

Using the fine side of a cheese grater, grate enough of the yellow part off the lemon's rind to make 1½ teaspoons; set the grated rind aside. Put the crustless bread in a large mixing bowl. Use the heel of your hand to press down and roll the same lemon you just used repeatedly over the kitchen counter to soften the inside; cut the lemon in half and squeeze both halves over the bread; remove any seeds. Pour the water over the bread and let soak for 10 minutes.

Hold the soaked bread in a ball between your hands and gently squeeze out any excess liquid; repeat the squeezing a few times and discard the excess liquid; use your hands to squish the bread into small pieces. Mix in the beaten egg, Parmesan cheese, parsley, garlic, and pepper; stir in the grated lemon rind. Break the ground beef into bits and use your hands to lightly toss it into the bread mixture, but don't overwork the mixture. Remove the sausage meat from its casings by squeezing it out the ends. Break it into bits and then gently but thoroughly mix it into the ground beef mixture. Shape the mixture into 1-inch balls. Put the meatballs in a single layer on a 10- by 15-inch or similar baking sheet; cover with plastic wrap and refrigerate until ready to use—for up to 1½ days.

To Cook an Individual Serving

Unwrap the stick of butter and put it on a plate. Cut the butter into 4 equal pieces and let it soften at room temperature.

Bring a large pot of water to a rapid boil; add one fourth of the box of spaghetti and boil following the package directions. (If you have a 16-ounce box of spaghetti, use one eighth of the box for each serving.)

Put 3 tablespoons of the olive oil in an 8-inch skillet over medium-high heat. When the oil is hot, add one fourth of the refrigerated meatballs and fry, stirring and turning now and then, so that the meatballs cook and become brown on all sides. After 10 minutes, cut a meatball in half to check for any traces of pink; cook longer, if necessary, or else remove the skillet from the heat.

When the spaghetti is done, rinse it in a colander under hot tap water, drain thoroughly and put it into a shallow soup bowl; mix in one of the softened butter chunks, add salt and Parmesan cheese to taste, and toss well. Using a slotted spoon, place the meatballs (but not their cooking oil) on top of the spaghetti and serve.

To Cook Multiple Servings

Cook following the directions above, using one fourth of the raw spaghetti, refrigerated meatballs, and butter for each serving. Use only 2 tablespoons of olive oil for each serving in an accommodating skillet if you are cooking more than 2 portions together.

NOTE: Once cooked, any extras of these meatballs freeze well.

Country-Style Barbecued Ribs

Serves 4
Cooking Time: 15 minutes

About 5 pounds country-style
  ribs or the equivalent of 8
  good-size ribs

Pepper to taste
2 cups bottled barbecue sauce
Coleslaw (page 216)

Preheat the oven to 350 degrees. Set a wire rack in an 8- by 12-by 2-inch or similar baking pan. Rub pepper into each rib on both sides; brush each rib on both sides with ¼ cup of the barbecue sauce. Place the ribs, side by side, on the rack. Cover the pan snugly with aluminum foil so that no air can escape and bake for 1½ hours. When you remove the pan from the oven, take care not to tip it as there will be a lot of very hot rendered fat in the pan. Loosen the aluminum foil to let the steam escape; then cool the ribs, partially covered, until they are lukewarm.

When the ribs are cool, remove the foil and lift the rack of ribs out of the pan; discard all of the fat in the pan and return the ribs to the pan without the rack. Pour the remaining 1¾ cups of barbecue sauce over the ribs and use your fingertips or a brush to generously cover each rib on all sides with the sauce. Cover the pan with a new piece of aluminum foil and refrigerate until ready to use—for up to 2 days.

Prepare the Coleslaw and apportion it into 4 small dishes; cover with plastic wrap or aluminum foil and refrigerate along with the ribs.

To Cook an Individual Serving

Let a portion of the coleslaw come to room temperature. Preheat the broiler in your oven. Transfer 2 of the ribs to a shallow baking pan and brush them generously with some of the barbecue sauce from the pan. Set the pan on the rack closest to the broiler. Broil for 7 to 10 minutes on one side, or until the sauce bubbles and browns; turn the ribs over, brush with more sauce, and broil for another 4 to 5 minutes, or until the sauce bubbles. Serve with the coleslaw and, if you wish, buttered corn.

To Cook Multiple Servings

Cook following the directions above, using 2 ribs and 1 portion of coleslaw for each serving.

Pork Balls with Ginger-Orange Glaze

Serves 4 to 5
Cooking Time: 10 minutes

MEATBALLS

2 large eggs
2 tablespoons soy sauce
¾ cup fine dry bread crumbs
1 bunch scallions, chopped
  (about 1 cup)
1 8-ounce can water chestnuts,
  drained and finely chopped
2 pounds lean ground pork
  with no seasoning

GLAZE

⅓ cup cornstarch
¼ cup sugar
1 tablespoon ground ginger
1 13¾-ounce can regular-
  strength beef broth
1 cup strained fresh orange
  juice
⅓ cup distilled white vinegar
2 tablespoons soy sauce

ACCOMPANIMENT
Rice Pilaf (page 213)

Preheat the oven to 500 degrees.

Partially beat the eggs in a large mixing bowl; stir in the soy sauce and bread crumbs. Then set aside for 10 minutes to let the bread crumbs absorb the eggs. Stir in the scallions and water chestnuts and use your hands to thoroughly blend in the pork, but do not overwork the mixture. Shape the mixture into ¾- to 1-inch meatballs and place them, sides gently touching, in a 10- by 15-inch baking pan. Bake, uncovered, for 15 minutes. Be careful to stand back when you open the oven door because there will be quite a build-up of heat. Cut a meatball in half to be certain that no pink remains in the center; if there is, return the pan to the oven for another 5 minutes and then check again. If there is any excess grease in the pan, drain it off and then let the meatballs cool to room temperature. When cool, cover with aluminum foil and refrigerate until ready to use—for up to 2 days.

Make the glaze also ahead of time: In a heavy, preferably non-stick saucepan, mix the cornstarch, sugar, and ginger together; gradually stir in the beef broth to make a smooth mixture. Then stir in the remaining glaze ingredients. Put the saucepan over medium heat and stir constantly (cornstarch likes to stick to the pot) until bubbly and thickened. Remove the glaze from the heat and let it cool to room temperature. Cover and refrigerate until ready to use. The glaze will also keep easily for several days.

Once the meatballs and glaze are prepared, make the Rice Pilaf; then cool and refrigerate it as directed until ready to use—for up to 2 days.

To Cook an Individual Serving

Measure 1½ cups of meatballs into a small saucepan or skillet and add ⅔ cup of the glaze. Warm gently over medium heat until the meatballs are hot throughout and the sauce begins to bubble, about 10 minutes. Heat up the made-in-advance Rice Pilaf following the directions on page 214. Serve the glazed meatballs over a bed of the pilaf.

To Cook Multiple Servings

Heat the meatballs in their original pan, uncovered, in a preheated 400-degree oven for 8 to 10 minutes, or until they sizzle. In the meantime, heat the glaze in its saucepan, stirring over medium heat until it bubbles. At the same time, heat up the made-in-advance rice pilaf following the directions on page 214. Put the hot meatballs in a serving dish and stir in the hot glaze to coat them. Serve the meatballs over beds of the pilaf.

Kulebiaka Pastries

Serves 4
Cooking Time: 20 minutes

These flaky-crusted, oval pastries filled with salmon, pilaf, mushrooms, and dill were once a delicacy made for the Czar of Russia.

2 cups all-purpose flour
12 tablespoons (1 ½ sticks)
　cold butter
4 tablespoons vegetable
　shortening, chilled
4 to 5 tablespoons ice-cold
　water
⅓ cup long-grain converted
　rice
1 cup regular-strength canned
　chicken broth
¼ teaspoon salt
⅛ teaspoon pepper

8 ounces fresh mushrooms,
　thinly sliced
½ lemon
3 tablespoons snipped fresh
　dillweed, or 1 tablespoon
　dried dill
1 15½-ounce can red salmon
1 ½ cups chopped onion
1 large egg yolk
1 tablespoon heavy or light
　cream or milk
1 pint sour cream

Make the pastry: Put the flour in a mixing bowl. Cut 8 tablespoons
of the butter into bits and add them to the flour along with the
shortening. Working quickly, use a pastry cutter to work the butter
into the flour to get a coarse, lumpy meal; don't let the butter melt
or even soften. Still working speedily, drizzle 4 tablespoons of the
ice-cold water into the mixture; toss quickly with your fingertips or
2 forks. If the mixture looks as if it will all gather into a ball, do so;
if it needs several more teaspoons of water followed by another
tossing, do that; then gather the mixture into a non-sticky ball of
dough. Still working swiftly so that the butter won't melt, cut the
ball of dough into 4 and then 8 equal-size pieces. Place them, apart,
on a large baking sheet and flatten them out with the heel of your
hand into crude ovals about 4 by 5 inches across. Quickly cover the
ovals with plastic wrap and refrigerate for 1 hour while you make the
filling.

　Melt 2 teaspoons of the remaining butter in a small saucepan over
medium-high heat. Add the rice and stir constantly until the butter
begins to bubble and the rice appears somewhat translucent. Add
the broth, salt, and pepper and bring to a gentle boil; then cover
and simmer for 20 minutes. Turn off the heat and let stand, still

covered, for 10 more minutes so all the broth will be absorbed. Uncover and set aside to cool.

Melt 1 tablespoon of the remaining butter in a skillet over medium heat; add the mushrooms and sauté for about 5 minutes, or until they are limp and juicy. Pour the skillet's contents into a big mixing bowl and stir in the juice from half a lemon (that's about 2 tablespoons) and the dill. Drain the salmon and remove and discard all the skin and bones. Flake the salmon meat, in clumps rather than shreds, into the bowl of mushrooms.

Melt 1 tablespoon of the remaining butter in the skillet over medium to medium-high heat; add the onion and sauté for 8 to 10 minutes, or until it is soft and no liquid remains. Add the onion to the bowl of mushrooms and salmon; then gently mix in the rice. Taste to see if the mixture needs salt. Cover and refrigerate.

Use ½ tablespoon of butter to grease two 12- by 15-inch baking sheets; set them aside. Place one of the dough ovals on a floured surface (keep the others refrigerated) and roll it into a larger oval of about 5 by 8 inches. Quickly place this oval on 1 of the buttered baking sheets and refrigerate it; repeat this process for 3 more ovals. Put equal amounts of filling, each about 1 heaping cup, on each of the rolled-out ovals, leaving a 1-inch margin; wet the dough margins with watered fingertips. Roll a remaining refrigerated dough oval into a 5- by 8-inch oval and drape it over the filling to cover it completely; fold up both dough margins together and crimp at an angle to seal the oval. Repeat so that all 4 filled ovals are sealed. Refrigerate, lightly covered, for at least 1 hour, or until ready to use —for up to 2 days.

After an hour (or else just before dinnertime) cut a 1-inch hole in the top of each pastry oval. Combine the egg yolk and cream and brush generously over each pastry.

To Cook an Individual Serving

Use 2 metal spatulas to transfer 1 kulebiaka pastry to a buttered baking sheet or pan. Bake in a preheated 450-degree oven for 20 minutes, or until the crust is golden. Serve topped with lots of sour cream.

To Cook Multiple Servings

Bake following the directions above, without transferring the pastries to another baking sheet.

Baked Fish Florentine

Serves 4
Cooking Time: 5 to 8 minutes

1 10-ounce package frozen
  chopped spinach, thawed
1 3-ounce package cream
  cheese and chives, softened
¼ teaspoon salt
Several dashes of pepper

Juice of ½ lemon
7 tablespoons butter
1 cup fine dry bread crumbs
8 baby sole fillets (use 2 12-
  ounce packages), thawed
  enough to separate

Boil the thawed spinach in ¼ cup of water for 2 minutes; don't overcook it. Working quickly to prevent heat loss, drain the spinach in a strainer; toss well and then press out all the excess water with the back of a tablespoon; return the drained spinach to its cooking pot. Pinch the package of softened cream cheese into pieces and stir them into the spinach until the mixture is smooth; stir in the salt, pepper, and lemon juice. Put the spinach mixture, still in its cooking pot, uncovered, in the refrigerator to cool.

Melt 6 tablespoons of the butter in a skillet over medium-high heat; add the bread crumbs and heat and stir for 3 to 4 minutes, or until the crumbs are lightly toasted. Spread the buttered crumbs on a dinner plate and set it aside, uncovered.

Grease a 10- by 15-inch baking pan with the remaining tablespoon of butter. Place 4 of the sole fillets, skin side down, in the pan. Spread equal portions of the spinach mixture on top of each fillet leaving a ¼-inch margin. Top each fillet with a similarly-sized fillet, skin side up. Sprinkle each generously with the buttered crumbs; very gently, press the crumbs onto the fish with your fingertips. Cover the pan loosely with plastic wrap. Refrigerate until ready to use—for up to 1½ days.

To Cook an Individual Serving

Preheat the oven to 500 degrees. Generously butter a shallow pan that will accommodate 1 double-fillet portion. Use a wide metal spatula, or 2 spatulas, to transfer the portion to the buttered pan. Bake for 5 to 8 minutes without turning, or until the bottom fillet is flaky and the crumbs are amber-brown.

To Cook Multiple Servings

Cook following the directions above. Use a pan that accommodates 2 portions; or remove 1 portion and cook 3 portions in the original buttered pan.

Fish Kabob Roll-Ups

Serves 4
Cooking Time: 10 minutes

16 tablespoons (2 sticks)
  butter, softened
1½ to 2 pounds sole fillets
¼ cup all-purpose flour
½ cup fine dry bread crumbs
2 tablespoons minced fresh
  parsley leaves, or 2
  teaspoons dried parsley
  flakes

2 tablespoons very finely
  minced onion
1 tablespoon fresh lemon juice
4 dashes of salt
4 dashes of pepper
1 lemon

4 8- to 12-inch-long bamboo
  or metal skewers

Several hours beforehand, set the sticks of butter out at room temperature to soften; cut 1 of the sticks in half while it is still solid.

Cut the fish fillets lengthwise into strips about 2 inches wide (there is usually a natural cutting line to follow on each fillet). Dust both sides of each fish strip in the flour; set the strips aside, skin side down and uncovered, while you make the filling.

In a mixing bowl, combine 12 tablespoons of the softened butter with the bread crumbs, parsley, onion, lemon juice, salt, and pepper. Blend the mixture into a uniform paste with the back of a tablespoon.

Put a strip of fish before you, skin side down; put a portion of the butter-paste in a thin line down the center of the strip of fish. Starting with the thick end first, roll up the fish, jelly roll fashion, and then thread it on a skewer. Do this for all the fish strips, using generous but equal amounts of butter-paste and dividing the roll-ups equally among the 4 skewers. Place the completed skewers in a large shallow pan. Dot each skewer with 1 tablespoon of the remaining softened butter; use your fingers to gently spread the butter over each fish roll-up. Squeeze the juice of the lemon over the skewered roll-ups. Cover the pan loosely with plastic wrap and refrigerate until ready to use—for up to 1½ days.

To Cook an Individual Serving

Preheat the oven to broil. Place 1 skewer of fish roll-ups in an accommodating shallow pan. Broil 6 inches away from the heat source for 5 minutes on one side; then carefully turn the skewer and continue broiling the roll-ups on the other side for 5 more minutes, or until the fish flakes at the center.

To Cook Multiple Servings

Cook following the directions above, using 1 skewer for each serving.

Seafood Chowder

Serves 4
Cooking Time: 7 to 10 minutes

8 slices bacon
3 medium-size onions, chopped
2 cups peeled potatoes cut into ½-inch cubes
2 tablespoons all-purpose flour
¾ cup instant mashed potato flakes
1 8-ounce bottle clam juice
1 10½-ounce can minced clams

1 cup water
1 cup milk
1 pound boneless cod, cut into 1½-inch chunks
2 tablespoons snipped fresh parsley leaves, or 2 teaspoons dried parsley flakes
¼ teaspoon pepper

In a 3-quart soup pot, slowly cook the bacon over medium to medium-high heat until it is well crisped; remove the bacon to a bowl and set it aside. Over high heat, use the bacon drippings in the pot to sauté the onions and potato cubes for about 2 to 3 minutes, or until the onions are limp but not brown. Remove the pot from the heat and immediately stir in the flour and the mashed potato flakes until they are dissolved. Gently stir in the clam juice, the canned clams and their juice, and all the remaining ingredients; crumble the reserved bacon and stir it into the soup pot as well. Cover and refrigerate until ready to use—for up to 1½ days.

To Cook an Individual Serving

Measure 2 cups of the raw chowder into a saucepan, preferably non-stick. Slowly bring to a boil over medium to medium-high heat, stirring frequently; cover and simmer for 7 to 10 minutes, or until the potatoes and fish are just tender. Turn the heat to very low, if necessary, and stir frequently to prevent sticking. Serve with a crisp tossed salad.

To Cook Multiple Servings

Cook following the directions above, using 2 cups of chowder for each serving.

≥ 2 ≤

INDIVIDUAL CASSEROLE DINNERS

Self-contained, one-serving casserole dinners can be preassembled, refrigerated, and then baked briefly when needed.

Creamy Chicken and Sausage Lasagnes

Chicken Florentine Casseroles

Chinese Chicken Casseroles

Salisbury Steak with Potatoes

Easy Enchilada Casseroles

Mini Pastitso Casseroles

Ham, Mushrooms, and Pasta in White Wine and Cheese Sauce

Ham, Potato, and Onion Casseroles

Spaghetti Baked in Clam Sauce

Fish Creole Casseroles

Steamed Fish Packets, Two Ways

Creamy Chicken and Sausage Lasagnes

Makes 4 servings
Cooking Time: 20 minutes

1¾ to 2 pounds chicken thighs
½ pound Italian sweet sausage
  (about 3 5- by 1-inch links)
4 tablespoons butter
4 tablespoons all-purpose flour
1 cup regular-strength canned
  chicken broth
1 cup milk
1 tablespoon minced fresh
  parsley leaves, or 1 teaspoon
  dried parsley flakes

½ teaspoon salt
⅛ teaspoon pepper
12 ounces whole milk
  mozzarella cheese
8 ounces raw lasagne noodles,
  (Use half of a 16-ounce
  box.)

4 oval mini-casserole aluminum
  foil pans (about 7 by 5 by 1
  inch)

Remove and discard the skin from the chicken thighs. Cut the meat off at both sides of the bones; cut the remaining meat off the bones; discard the bones. Use a mallet or a heavy frying pan to smash each piece of chicken flat to the point of shreds. Cut this chicken into, roughly, 1-inch pieces; set it aside.

Squeeze the sausage meat out of its casing and crumble it into a large frying pan. Sauté over medium heat until all the pink is gone. Add the chicken pieces and stir and sauté for about 10 minutes, or until no pink remains, but don't overcook the meat. Spoon out and reserve the fat from the pan. Set the meat mixture aside.

Make the sauce: Melt the butter in a saucepan (preferably one with a non-stick surface) over medium-low heat; do not let it brown. Blend in the flour with a wire whisk. Remove the pan from the heat and gradually stir in the chicken broth, blending it in, bit by bit; then stir in the milk, parsley, salt, and pepper. Return the pan to the heat; raise the heat to medium and cook, stirring frequently and patiently; stir more rapidly when the sauce begins to thicken, so that it won't stick to the bottom of the pan; lower the heat, if necessary. When the sauce has completely thickened and begins to bubble at the center, remove it from the heat. Reserve ⅓ cup of the sauce for use later and stir the remaining sauce into the meat mixture; set it aside.

Shred the mozzarella on the coarse side of a cheese grater; divide it first into 4 and then into 12 separate and somewhat equal piles on your work area. Nearby, set out the 4 mini-casserole pans; brush the pan bottoms and sides generously with the reserved fat from the chicken and sausage. Spread equal amounts of the sauce in the 4 pans.

Half of a 16-ounce box of lasagne noodles consists of 8 to 10 noodles; snap them in half and cook them following the package directions. Drain the noodles and then transfer them to a pot of cold water to chill.

Assemble the lasagnes in the following manner:

1. Layer each pan with one eighth of the lasagne noodles (about 1 ¼ full noodles for each pan).
2. Sprinkle each pan with its own pile of mozzarella.
3. Evenly spread one eighth of the meat mixture over the mozzarella in each pan, using your fingers, if necessary, to arrange it.
4. Repeat Steps 1, 2, and 3, above.
5. Lastly, cover the meat mixture in each pan with each of the remaining 4 piles of mozzarella. Cover each casserole with plastic wrap or aluminum foil and refrigerate until ready to use—for up to 2 days.

To Cook

Preheat the oven to 450 degrees. Bake, uncovered, for 20 minutes. To serve, either slide or invert onto a dinner plate.

Chicken Florentine Casseroles

Makes 4 servings
Cooking Time: 15 minutes

1 3½-pound whole chicken
1 9-ounce package frozen
   creamed spinach in a boil-in
   bag or plain chopped
   spinach in a boil-in bag plus
   2 tablespoons butter
3½ tablespoons butter
¾ cup long-grain converted
   rice

½ teaspoon salt
Pepper to taste
1 13¾-ounce can regular-
   strength chicken broth

4 oval mini-casserole aluminum
   foil pans (about 7 by 5 by 1
   inch) or 4 5-inch-round by
   2-inch-deep ramekins

Preheat the oven to 450 degrees.

Rinse out the chicken cavity. Put the chicken, breast side up, on a single layer of aluminum foil; wrap snugly and airtight. Put the wrapped chicken in a shallow baking pan and bake for 50 minutes. Put the hot pan of chicken—don't unwrap it—in the refrigerator and chill for 2 hours or overnight.

In the meantime, allow the boil-in bag of spinach to thaw (once thawed, you can return it to the refrigerator overnight), and make the following rice pilaf: Melt 1½ tablespoons of the butter in a heavy saucepan over medium heat. When it bubbles, stir in the rice, salt, and pepper and sauté, stirring frequently, until the rice takes on a slightly translucent quality. Don't let the kernels get brown or pop. Slowly stir in the chicken broth (if your can of broth contains 14½ ounces, add 1 more tablespoon of rice to the pot); bring to a boil over high heat; then cover and lower heat to maintain a steady simmer. Simmer for 20 to 25 minutes, or until nearly all the liquid has been absorbed. Turn off the heat and let the rice stand without removing the cover for 10 minutes. Remove the cover so that the rice can cool slightly; then divide the rice equally among the 4 pans. Cover with aluminum foil and refrigerate (overnight, if necessary) until the chicken has chilled.

When you unwrap the cooled chicken, you will find some jelled aspic and a fatty liquid; pour this off into a cup and refrigerate it; once chilled, you can discard the top layer of fat and use the aspic as rich chicken broth. Remove and discard all skin, fat, and bones from the chicken; use your fingers to separate the chicken meat into 1-inch-long shreds. Divide the chicken equally over the pans of rice. Distribute the spinach equally over the 4 pans, using your fingertips to spread it over and into all the chicken pieces. Place ½ tablespoon of butter, cut into bits, over the first pan; repeat for the remaining pans (if you are using plain spinach, double the amount of butter). Cover the pans with aluminum foil and refrigerate until ready to use —for up to 2 days.

To Cook

Bake, uncovered, in a preheated 475-degree oven for 15 minutes. To serve, slide the contents of the aluminum pan onto a dinner plate or serve straight from the ramekin.

Chinese Chicken Casseroles

Makes 4 servings
Cooking Time: 15 minutes

2 pounds chicken thighs
1 large egg white
1 tablespoon corn oil
2 teaspoons cornstarch
¼ teaspoon baking soda
¼ teaspoon soy sauce
1 10¾-ounce can condensed
   cream of chicken soup
½ cup mayonnaise
1 small onion
4 ounces fresh mushrooms

1 8-ounce can whole water
   chestnuts
3 celery stalks
1 3-ounce can chow mein
   noodles

4 oval mini-casserole aluminum
   foil pans (about 7 by 5 by 1
   inch) or 4 5-inch-round by
   2-inch-deep ramekins

Remove and discard the skin and bones from the chicken thighs; cut the meat into ½- to ¾-inch pieces. In a medium-size mixing bowl, lightly beat the egg white until foamy; blend in the corn oil, cornstarch, baking soda, and soy sauce. Add the chicken pieces to this mixture; stir until the pieces are coated on all sides and then set aside at room temperature for at least 10 minutes, preferably more.

In the meantime, combine the soup, mayonnaise, and 1 tablespoon of grated onion in a large mixing bowl; set aside. Slice the mushrooms into the thinnest possible slices and then chop them roughly (they will measure about 1½ cups). Mix the mushrooms into the soup-mayonnaise mixture. Drain off the liquid from the can of water chestnuts and chop the water chestnuts into ⅛-inch pieces. Mix them into the soup-mayonnaise mixture. Trim and then scrape the celery to get three 5-inch stalks or their equivalent; slice the celery on a diagonal to get the thinnest possible slices (they will measure about ⅔ cup) and set aside next to the chicken.

Using a 4-quart pot, bring 2 quarts of water to a steady boil over high heat. Add the chicken and the celery and cook, stirring now and then, lowering the heat, if necessary, for 45 seconds, or until the chicken is no longer pink; be careful not to overcook it. Drain the chicken and celery in a colander and mix them into the large bowl of ingredients. Then divide the mixture equally among the 4 pans. Sprinkle each casserole equally with chow mein noodles; cover

with plastic wrap or aluminum foil and refrigerate until ready to use
—for up to 3 days.

To Cook

Bake, uncovered, in a preheated 475-degree oven for 15 minutes.
To serve, invert the aluminum pan onto a dinner plate or serve
straight from the ramekin.

Salisbury Steak with Potatoes

Makes 4 servings
Cooking Time: 20 minutes

4 large potatoes or the
   equivalent of 4 portions of
   mashed potato flakes
Salt and pepper
3 tablespoons butter, melted
1 large egg
¼ cup milk
½ cup fine dry bread crumbs
1 small onion, either grated or
   very finely minced
2 tablespoons minced fresh
   parsley leaves, or 2
   teaspoons dried parsley
   flakes

1 pound ground beef
1 14¾-ounce can beef gravy
   or 2 10-ounce cans or 1 12-
   ounce jar

4 oval mini-casserole aluminum
   foil pans (about 7 by 5 by 1
   inch) or 4 5-inch-round by
   2-inch-deep ramekins

Peel and cut the potatoes into uniform, ¼-inch dice (about 4 to 5 cups); place in a bowl of cold water. Rinse the potatoes in a colander under cold running water to remove the starch; then let potatoes drain for 5 minutes; dry the bowl. Return the potatoes to the bowl and then sprinkle with the salt and pepper to taste. Pour on the melted butter and stir to coat the potatoes uniformly. Divide the potatoes equally among the 4 pans and set them aside.

In a mixing bowl, combine the egg and milk; stir in the bread crumbs and soak for 10 minutes. Stir in the onion and parsley and season with ½ teaspoon salt and ⅛ teaspoon pepper. Use your fingers to toss in and mix in the ground beef, but don't overwork the mixture.

Preheat the oven to 350 degrees. Tilt each one of the pans to drain out the excess water remaining in the potatoes. Shape the meat mixture into 4 flat, oval patties, each about 6 inches long (or into 5-inch round patties if you are using ramekins); place 1 patty on top of the potatoes in each pan. Bake, uncovered, for 40 minutes; remove the pans from the oven and allow them to cool. Pour the gravy equally over both the meat and potatoes in each pan. Cover the pans with aluminum foil and refrigerate until ready to use—for up to 3 days.

To Cook

Bake, uncovered, in a preheated 475-degree oven for 20 minutes. To serve, transfer the steak to a dinner plate, mix the gravy into the potatoes, and then transfer them to the plate next to the steak.

Variation:

TURKEY WITH POTATOES

Substitute 1 pound of ground raw turkey (either fresh or frozen and thawed) for the ground beef. Replace the beef gravy with either turkey or chicken gravy.

Easy Enchilada Casseroles

Makes 4 servings
Cooking Time: 15 minutes

There is no tricky rolling-up of tortillas in this recipe. Instead, the tortillas are snipped into noodle-like strips to make tasty casseroles.

12 ounces sharp Cheddar
   cheese
2 tablespoons all-purpose flour
3 tablespoons oil
1 cup chopped onion
2 garlic cloves, smashed and
   minced
1 4-ounce can mild green
   chiles (or the hotter
   jalapeño, if you prefer)
1 15-ounce can tomato sauce
¼ teaspoon sugar
½ teaspoon salt, optional

¼ teaspoon pepper
1 pound boneless chuck steak
¼ teaspoon ground cumin
12 6- or 7-inch-diameter corn
   tortillas

4 oval mini-casserole aluminum
   foil pans (about 7 by 5 by 1
   inch) or 4 foil roll-pans
   (about 8 by 5 inch) or 4
   5-inch-round by 2-inch-deep
   ramekins

Shred the cheese, about 3½ cups' worth, into a mixing bowl; add the flour and toss to coat the cheese. Measure out 1 heaping cup of cheese and set aside both the cup and the bowl of cheese.

Heat 2 tablespoons of the oil in a 10-inch skillet over medium-high heat; sauté the onion and garlic for 5 minutes, or until they are soft. Scrape the vegetables into a blender; add the chiles and their juices and blend at high speed until completely puréed. Pour the purée back into the skillet; then stir in the tomato sauce, sugar, salt, and pepper. Bring the sauce to a sort of splurting simmer over medium to medium-high heat; then turn the heat to medium-low and simmer, uncovered, for 5 minutes, stirring now and then. Remove the skillet from the heat and stir in the shredded cheese in the bowl until it has melted. Pour the sauce back into the bowl that held the cheese and set it aside. Rinse out the skillet.

Use a sharp knife to cut the steak lengthwise in half or into thirds so that you can slice the meat into thin, almost shred-like bits that are about 1 inch long. Heat the remaining tablespoon of oil in the skillet over medium-high heat and sauté the meat, stirring frequently, until the meat has lost its pink color; don't overcook it. Remove the skillet from the heat and drain off all the pan juices. While the skillet is still hot, season the meat with salt and pepper to taste; then stir in the cumin, 4 tablespoons of the sauce from the bowl, and the remaining cup of shredded cheese. Stir until the cheese has melted; then set aside.

Set out the 4 pans. Fold 1 tortilla in half and then lengthwise in half again. Holding the tortilla over the first pan, use scissors to cut it into thin, noodle-like strips ⅛ to ¼ inch wide. Spread the strips evenly over the bottom of the pan; repeat with the remaining tortillas and pans, using 1 tortilla for each pan. Put equal dollops of the meat mixture into each pan. Fill from the center out, to cover the tortilla strips, but don't expect to cover all the strips.

Next, take two tortillas, fold them in half together and lengthwise in half again; use scissors to snip them into strips to cover the meat in the first pan; repeat the process for each pan. Ladle equal amounts of the sauce over the strips in each pan. Use the back of a spoon to gently cover all the tortilla strips with sauce, working the sauce out to the corners of the pans. Cover the pans with aluminum foil and refrigerate until ready to use—for up to 2 days.

To Cook

Preheat the oven to 425 degrees. Bake the pan(s), uncovered, for 15 minutes, or until a knife inserted in the center comes out hot.

Mini Pastitso Casseroles

Makes 4 servings
Cooking Time: 20 minutes

1 pound ground beef
1 small onion, finely chopped
1 8-ounce can tomato sauce
½ teaspoon salt
Several dashes of pepper
2 teaspoons ground allspice
¼ teaspoon ground cinnamon
¼ teaspoon ground nutmeg
2½ cups elbow macaroni
4 tablespoons butter

3 large eggs
¾ cup grated Parmesan cheese
2 teaspoons all-purpose flour
¼ cup milk

4 oval mini-casserole aluminum
  foil pans (about 7 by 5 by 1
  inch) or 4 5-inch-round by
  2-inch-deep ramekins

Sauté the meat and the onion together in a frying pan over medium-high heat; when no pink remains, drain off all the excess fat. Lower the heat to medium and stir in the tomato sauce, salt, pepper, allspice, cinnamon, and nutmeg; simmer, uncovered, for 5 minutes, or until the sauce has thickened somewhat. Transfer the meat mixture to a dinner plate and refrigerate, uncovered, to hasten cooling.

Cook the macaroni following the package directions, using no more than the least boiling time recommended on the box. Drain the cooked macaroni in a colander; then rinse it thoroughly under cold running water and drain again for 10 minutes.

In the meantime, prepare the following: Melt the butter in a small saucepan and allow it to cool. Set out the 4 mini-casserole pans and brush the bottoms with a thin coating of the melted butter; set the rest of the butter aside. Beat 1 of the eggs in a large mixing bowl; use a rubber spatula to mix in the cooled meat mixture; scrape the whole thing back onto the dinner plate and set it aside.

When the macaroni has drained, beat another egg in the large mixing bowl; add 3 cups of cooked macaroni and stir well to coat the macaroni. Spread this eggy macaroni evenly among the 4 pans, using ¾ cup for each pan. Sprinkle each pan evenly with 1 table-spoon of the Parmesan cheese. Spread the meat mixture equally over the macaroni in each pan right up to the pan edges.

Pour the remaining macaroni into the large mixing bowl. Stir in the melted butter to coat it well and then stir in the remaining Parmesan cheese to coat the macaroni. Spread this mixture equally over the meat layer in each pan, separating the macaroni with your fingers to get an even layer over each.

Separate the last egg, putting the white into a clean dry mixing bowl; reserve the yolk. Beat the egg white to a foamy froth; then beat in the flour. Gently stir in the egg yolk and then the milk. Spoon this equally over the top macaroni layer in each pan. Cover with aluminum foil and refrigerate until ready to use—for up to 1 day.

To Cook

Preheat the oven to 450 degrees. Bake the casseroles, uncovered, for 20 minutes. Serve in the pan or ramekin or invert onto a dinner plate.

Ham, Mushrooms, and Pasta in White Wine and Cheese Sauce

Makes 4 servings
Cooking Time: 15 minutes

12 ounces fresh mushrooms
8 tablespoons (1 stick) butter
½ cup dry white wine
Pepper
12 ounces boiled ham, thinly
    sliced
1 small onion
2 tablespoons all-purpose flour
1 ½ cups light cream or
    half-and-half

8 ounces Monterey Jack
    cheese, shredded (about 2 ½
    cups)
8 ounces mostaccioli or ziti or
    any other 1 ½-inch-long,
    ¼-inch-wide macaroni

4 oval mini-casserole aluminum
    foil pans (about 7 by 5 by 1
    inch) or 4 5-inch-round by
    2-inch-deep ramekins

Cut the mushrooms into ¼- to ½-inch-thick slices. Heat 3 table-spoons of the butter in a skillet over medium heat. Add the mush-rooms and sauté for about 5 minutes, or until they are limp and their juices appear. Scrape the mushrooms into a small bowl and add the wine and several dashes of pepper; set the bowl aside.

Cut the ham in half lengthwise; stack one pile on top of the other and then slice the ham into thin, short julienne strips. You will need about 2¾ cups. Chop the small onion to get about ¼ cup. Melt 1 tablespoon of the butter in the same skillet over medium to medium-high heat. Add the ham and onion and sauté for about 10 minutes, or until the ham liquid has evaporated. Transfer the mixture to a big mixing bowl and set it aside.

Melt 2 tablespoons of the butter in the same skillet over medium heat. Remove the skillet from the heat and stir in the flour until blended. Return the skillet to the heat; as soon as the flour-butter mixture bubbles, gradually stir in the cream plus all the liquid from the bowl of mushrooms. Continue to stir and cook until the sauce has thickened. Stir in the shredded cheese and cook until it has melted; then remove the skillet from the heat.

Cook the mostaccioli following the package directions; drain in a colander; submerge the pasta in cold water until cool and then drain thoroughly.

Add the mushrooms and cheese sauce to the bowl of ham and mix well. Then gently mix in the pasta. Use the last 2 tablespoons of butter to generously grease the 4 pans. Evenly distribute the mixture among the pans and cover each with aluminum foil. Refrigerate until ready to use—for up to 2 days.

To Cook

Preheat the oven to 425 degrees. Loosen the foil on the pan so that it is loose and not sealed. Bake for 15 minutes, or until a knife inserted in the center comes out hot.

Variation:

WITHOUT WINE

If you have children who don't like wine in their food, omit it and increase the cream by ½ cup.

Ham, Potato, and Onion Casseroles

Makes 4 servings
Cooking Time: 20 minutes

3 medium-size onions
8 tablespoons (1 stick) butter
4 large potatoes (about 2
  pounds total weight)
Salt and pepper to taste
12 ounces boiled ham, cut into
  thin julienne strips (about 2
  cups packed)

½ cup heavy cream

4 oval mini-casserole aluminum
  foil pans (about 7 by 5 by 1
  inches) or 4 5-inch-round by
  2-inch-deep ramekins

Peel the onions and cut each of them in half. Slice each half into
paper-thin half-circles. Heat 2 tablespoons of the butter in a large
frying pan over medium-high heat. Separate the onions into half-
rings and sauté them gently, tossing them with 2 spoons. In 10 to
15 minutes, when the onions are limp and stringy but not yet brown,
transfer them to a dinner plate and set them aside.

Melt 2 tablespoons of the butter in the frying pan. Brush the pans
with the butter being especially generous at the sides; set the pans
aside.

Peel the potatoes; use the single-slice side of a cheese grater or
use a food processor to cut them into thin but not paper-thin slices.
As they are sliced, put the slices into a bowl of cold water. When all
the potatoes are sliced, rinse them repeatedly in cold water to remove the excess starch. Spread the slices over lengths of paper
towels; cover them with more paper towels and pat gently to absorb
the excess water. Melt the remaining 4 tablespoons of butter in a
frying pan over medium-high heat. When it bubbles, add the potato
slices and sauté, stirring constantly with 2 spoons, for about 5 minutes, or until the potatoes have lost some of their stiffness and they
just begin to become sticky; set the pan aside.

Assemble each of the casserole pans in the following manner:
Layer one eighth of the potatoes followed by one eighth of the
onions in each pan. Sprinkle with salt and pepper to taste and cover
the seasoned onions with one quarter of the ham; then cover the
ham with one eighth of the potatoes. Drizzle 2 tablespoons of cream

over each pan and sprinkle again with salt and pepper. Cover each pan with plastic wrap, pressing it directly onto the top layer of potatoes. Refrigerate until ready to use—for up to 1½ days.

To Cook

Preheat the oven to 500 degrees. Bake, uncovered, for 20 minutes. To serve, invert the contents of the aluminum pans onto a dinner plate or serve directly from the ramekins.

Spaghetti Baked in Clam Sauce

Makes 4 servings
Cooking Time: 15 minutes

3 8-ounce bottles clam juice
2 6½-ounce cans minced clams
2 cups water
8 tablespoons (1 stick) butter
4 tablespoons olive oil
1 16-ounce box regular (#8)
    spaghetti
1 to 4 garlic cloves
½ lemon

2 tablespoons minced fresh
    parsley leaves, or 1 teaspoon
    dried parsley flakes
Salt to taste, optional

4 oval mini-casserole aluminum
    foil pans (about 7 by 5 by 1
    inch) or 4 5-inch-round by
    2-inch-deep ramekins

Vigorously shake the bottles of clam juice; pour their contents into a large, preferably non-stick, pot. Open the canned clams and drain their juice into a measuring cup using the can lid to squeeze out every bit of juice; set the clams aside. If necessary, add enough water to the cup to measure exactly 1 cup; pour this into the pot. Add 2 cups of water to the pot so you have 6 cups of liquid in the pot. Add 2 tablespoons of the butter and 1 tablespoon of the oil to the pot. Open the box of spaghetti and break all the spaghetti in half, placing it in the pot as you do. Cover the pot and bring the liquid to a boil over high heat, stirring frequently to prevent sticking. Once the liquid is boiling, lower the heat to maintain a steady simmer and, at frequent intervals, continue to uncover and stir the spaghetti. Simmer in this fashion for the shortest time that the package directions specify, until the liquid—it will be very gummy looking—has been almost all absorbed. Cover the pot; listen for the simmer to return and then remove the pot from the heat. Let the pot sit, covered, for exactly 10 minutes—no more—then remove the cover to prevent any further cooking.

While the spaghetti is sitting, make the following sauce: In a small frying pan over medium heat, heat the remaining 6 tablespoons of butter and the remaining 3 tablespoons of olive oil. Peel and then smash 1 to 4 garlic cloves, depending on your taste for it, with the flat side of a knife; then mince the garlic very finely. When the butter and oil begin to bubble, add the garlic and the 2 cans of drained clams; return to a bubbly simmer and sauté until the garlic is limp and the clams just begin to pop.

Pour the sauce on top of the spaghetti; squeeze the lemon juice over it and add the parsley. Stir to distribute everything evenly. Taste to see if you want any salt; then divide the mixture equally among the 4 pans. Let cool slightly; then cover with plastic wrap or aluminum foil and refrigerate until ready to use—for up to 3 days.

To Cook

Preheat the oven to 450 degrees. Bake, uncovered, for 15 minutes. To serve, slide or invert onto a dinner plate.

Fish Creole Casseroles

Makes 4 servings
Cooking Time: 15 minutes

4 ½ tablespoons butter
¾ cup long-grain converted
    rice
1 teaspoon salt
Pepper
1 13¾-ounce can regular-
    strength chicken broth
1 cup chopped onion
½ cup scraped celery cut into
    thin diagonal slices
2 large garlic cloves, smashed
    and minced
1 1-pound can whole tomatoes
    (2 cups)
½ can tomato paste (about ¼
    cup)

¾ cup water
1 tablespoon Worcestershire
    sauce
2 teaspoons chili powder
½ teaspoon sugar
½ teaspoon Tabasco sauce
1 pound ¾-inch-thick fish,
    such as cod, pollack, or
    whiting

4 oval mini-casserole aluminum
    foil pans (about 7 by 5 by 1
    inch) or 4 5-inch-round by
    2-inch-deep ramekins

Make a rice pilaf: Melt 1½ tablespoons of the butter in a heavy saucepan over medium heat. When it bubbles, stir in the rice, ½ teaspoon of salt, and some pepper and sauté, stirring frequently, until the rice takes on a slightly translucent quality; don't let the kernels get brown or pop. Slowly stir in the chicken broth (if your can of broth contains 14½ ounces, add 1 more tablespoon of rice to the pot); bring to a boil over high heat; then cover and lower the heat to maintain a steady simmer. Simmer for 20 to 25 minutes, or until nearly all the liquid has been absorbed. Turn off the heat and let the rice stand without removing the cover for 10 minutes; then remove the cover so that the rice can cool slightly.

While the rice cooks, melt the remaining 3 tablespoons of butter in a frying pan over medium-high heat. Add the onion, celery, and garlic and sauté until the vegetables are limp but not brown, about 3 to 4 minutes. Pour the tomatoes into a mixing bowl and use your hands to squish them into small pieces. Stir the tomatoes into the frying pan and add the tomato paste, water, Worcestershire sauce, chili powder, ½ teaspoon salt, sugar, and Tabasco sauce. Lower the heat and simmer, uncovered, stirring now and then, for 30 minutes, or until no longer soupy.

When the rice is done and slightly cooled, divide it equally among the 4 pans. Cut the fish into 1½-inch chunks and spread them equally over the rice in the 4 pans; then refrigerate.

When the creole sauce is done, ladle equal amounts of the hot sauce over the fish in each pan; spread the sauce into an even layer. Allow the pans to cool at room temperature for 10 minutes; then cover them with aluminum foil and refrigerate until ready to use— for up to 1½ days.

To Cook

Preheat the oven to 500 degrees. Bake, uncovered, for 15 minutes. To serve, slide the contents of each aluminum pan onto a dinner plate or serve straight from the ramekin.

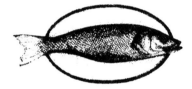

Steamed Fish Packets, Two Ways

Makes 4 servings
Cooking Time: 7 to 14 minutes

1 pound thin boneless fish fillets, such as sole,
    flounder, or perch
4 teaspoons corn oil
Your choice of flavoring (ingredients below)

Aluminum foil

PEAPODS AND WATER
CHESTNUTS

1 8-ounce can whole water
    chestnuts, drained and sliced
    paper-thin
1 6-ounce box frozen pea
    pods, thawed and drained
2 tablespoons corn oil
2 tablespoons butter, melted
1 ½ teaspoons soy sauce
⅛ teaspoon ground ginger

MUSHROOMS WITH DILL

4 tablespoons butter
8 ounces fresh mushrooms,
    thinly sliced (about 3 ½
    cups)
1 ½ teaspoons snipped fresh
    dillweed, or ½ teaspoon
    dried dill
Salt and pepper to taste

Separate the fish fillets into 4 equal portions; select the thickest piece; use a ruler to measure it at its thickest point; make a note of the measurement. Tear off 4 generous lengths of aluminum foil (each about 16 inches) which, when wrapped, will accommodate each fish portion arranged in a single layer. Brush each foil length with 1 teaspoon of oil leaving margins un-oiled. Place a fish portion, skin side down, in a single layer at the center of each piece of foil; add either the Pea Pods with Water Chestnuts or Mushrooms with Dill mixture following the directions below.

Wrap the fish and their accompaniment airtight but somewhat loosely at the top so that steam can accumulate within the packet when it cooks. Tape the note you made of your fish's thickness to one of the packets. Place the packets in a single layer on a baking sheet and refrigerate until ready to use—for up to 1 ½ days.

To Cook

Place an unwrapped packet on a shallow pan or baking sheet. Bake in a preheated 500-degree oven, allowing 7 minutes for every ¼-inch thickness of your fish (i.e.: ¼-inch-thick fish, such as sole and flounder, would bake 7 minutes; ½-inch fish, like perch, would bake 14 minutes).

To serve, remove the packet from the oven; unwrap, being careful of the escaping steam, and slide the contents onto a dinner plate.

Fish with Pea Pods and Water Chestnuts

Top the fish portion on each length of foil with equal amounts of water chestnuts and then top with pea pods. Combine the remaining 4 ingredients in a jar. Cover and shake well. Drizzle 1 tablespoon over each portion and wrap as directed.

Fish with Mushrooms and Dill

Melt 2 tablespoons of the butter in a frying pan. Add the mushrooms and sauté until they are just barely tender; remove the pan from the heat and allow to cool slightly.

Dot each fish portion on its length of foil with ½ tablespoon of butter. Sprinkle each portion with equal portions of the dill; then sprinkle with salt and pepper. Use a slotted spoon to place equal portions of the mushrooms over each portion; do not use the liquid. Wrap as directed.

⚘ 3 ⚘

FREEZER-TO-OVEN
15-MINUTE DINNERS

Always on hand, here are ready-made meals that go directly from your freezer to the oven to the table in 15 minutes or less.

Freezer-to-Oven Fried Wontons

Freezer-to-Oven Szechuan Burritos

Freezer-to-Oven Chicken Sticks

Freezer-to-Oven Macedonian Meat Patties

Freezer-to-Oven Fresh Salmon Cakes with Mushrooms and Dill

Freezer-to-Oven Batter-Dipped Fish Sticks

Freezer-to-Oven Spinach and Feta Fillo Triangles

Other Freezer-to-Oven Recipes from This Book

Freezer-to-Oven Fried Wontons

Makes about 60; or 7 to 10 servings
Cooking Time: 12 minutes

These are easier to make than you might think and well worth the effort when you see how fast your whole family eats them. Fresh wonton wrappers are sold in Oriental markets and often in the produce section of the supermarket.

1 1-pound package 3½-inch-square wonton wrappers	2 teaspoons cornstarch
1¼ pounds ground pork, no spices or flavorings added	⅛ teaspoon ground ginger
2 scallions, chopped	2 tablespoons soy sauce
1 6-ounce can water chestnuts, drained and finely chopped	Salt to taste
	About 3 cups oil for frying

Let the wonton wrappers stand, still wrapped, at room temperature for 1 hour before using. In the meantime, sauté the pork in a large skillet over medium-high heat for about 5 minutes, or until it has lost its pink color; break up the meat as it cooks. Drain off all the excess fat. Return the skillet to the heat and stir in the scallions and water chestnuts; turn the heat to medium-low and continue to sauté for 5 minutes more. Blend together 1 teaspoon of the cornstarch, the ginger, and soy sauce and drizzle this mixture over the meat in the skillet. Mix well and cook for 1 minute; then remove the skillet from the heat. Taste to see if you want any salt; then let the pork filling cool, uncovered.

In a measuring cup, make a sealing solution for the wontons by combining the remaining 1 teaspoon of cornstarch with ⅛ cup of cold water; stir to dissolve the cornstarch and then add enough very hot tap water to measure 1 cup; set it aside. Set a baking sheet and either a non-terrycloth towel or a length of plastic wrap near your work surface.

To assemble the first wonton:

1. Place a single wonton wrapper in front of you with the point of the square facing you.

2. Use a small paint brush or your fingertip to moisten the 4 edges with the prepared sealing solution.
3. Put 1 teaspoon of filling at the center of the wrapper. Take the point of the wrapper that is facing you and fold it over the filling to its opposite point. You now have a triangle whose longest (folded) side faces you. Press the triangle's united edges together to seal.
4. Dip the tips at each end of the longest (folded) side into the sealing solution. Pull these two ends together toward you and pinch the tips together. The resulting wonton will remind you of a giant tortellini or else a bit like a fancy-folded dinner napkin.
5. Place the wonton on the baking sheet and cover. Repeat this process for all the wrappers. After you get the hang of it, try an assembly line of 6 at a time.

Pour enough oil in a 10-inch skillet to make a depth of ¾ inch. Heat over medium-high heat until hot enough to pop a drop of water flicked into it. Add 10 wontons, plump side down, and fry until puffed, crisp, and golden brown on both sides, turning the wontons when necessary with a slotted spoon. Drain on paper towels. Repeat for all the wontons and then allow them all to cool.

Transfer the cooled wontons back to the baking sheet; cover loosely with plastic wrap and freeze for several hours, or until solid. Package in 2 large freezer bags; label with this page number and return to the freezer.

To Cook

Preheat the oven to 350 degrees. Allow 6 to 8 wontons for each serving. Place the frozen wontons on an ungreased baking pan (or a larger baking sheet for multiple servings) at least ½ inch apart. Bake for 12 minutes. Serve plain or with hot mustard or sweet-and-sour dipping sauces.

Variations:

WONTON SOUP

Rather than frying all the newly wrapped wontons, set some aside on a baking sheet lined with plastic wrap; allow 4 wontons for each serving of soup. Freeze the sheet of wontons, uncovered, for several hours, or until solid; then transfer them to a freezer bag; label it with this page number and return to the freezer.

To Cook an Individual Serving of Wonton Soup

Bring 1¼ cups of regular strength canned chicken broth and an optional tablespoon of cooked pork, cut into julienne matchsticks, to a boil in a small saucepan over medium-high heat. Add 4 frozen wontons, plus 1 or 2 leaves of fresh, stemless spinach (also optional). Return the broth to a boil; cover the pan and turn the heat to medium-low. Simmer for 5 minutes, or until the wontons are puffed and floating. Serve in a bowl garnished with a light sprinkling of chopped scallions or chives.

To Cook Multiple Servings of Wonton Soup

Cook following the directions above, multiplying the ingredients accordingly. When adding the frozen wontons, drop them in one at a time, waiting a few moments between each addition so as not to completely stop the broth from simmering.

Freezer-to-Oven Szechuan Burritos

Serves 4
Cooking Time: 15 minutes

Deliciously tender, fragrantly spiced pork slices make the filling for these crisp, fried rolls.

1 ½ pounds whole pork
   tenderloin
¼ cup soy sauce
¼ cup light corn syrup
2 medium garlic cloves,
   smashed and finely minced
2 tablespoons chopped
   scallions
2 ½ tablespoons distilled white
   vinegar
1 tablespoon sugar
2 teaspoons shredded orange
   rind

Strained juice of 1 orange
¼ teaspoon ground ginger
⅛ teaspoon anise seed,
   measured then crushed
1/16 teaspoon ground cinnamon
8 8-inch-diameter flour tortillas
2 or 3 cups oil for frying

8 toothpicks
1 medium-size plastic freezer
   bag or a plastic bread bag

Put the pork, probably in 2 pieces, in a heavy small-to-medium-size saucepan; curl the pieces around so that they both lay flat in the pan. In a mixing bowl, combine the next 11 ingredients (through the cinnamon); pour the mixture over the pork. Set the saucepan, uncovered, over medium heat and wait patiently until it comes to a steady boil; cover the pan, lower the heat slightly, and simmer for 15 minutes, lowering the heat as necessary. Turn the pork over and simmer, covered, for another 15 minutes. Remove the saucepan from the heat, uncover, and allow the pork to cool to room temperature —about 1 hour—turning the pieces after 30 minutes.

Remove the pork to a cutting board; set the saucepan of juices over medium heat. Use a sharp knife to slice the pork on a slight diagonal into thin, ⅛-inch-thick slices; set them aside. Raise the heat under the saucepan to high; let the juices within come to a boil and continue boiling, uncovered, for 8 to 10 minutes, or until the juices are thickened and syrupy. (The thickening will happen quickly toward the end of the allotted time, so be sure to stir the mixture frequently then.) Remove the pan from the heat and stir the mixture down until it stops bubbling. Using 2 spoons, gently stir in the pork slices, half at a time, so that they are all coated. Cover the saucepan and let it cool to room temperature.

Steam the first tortilla on a wire rack placed above a pan of boiling water; turn once so that the tortilla becomes soft and pliable on each side. Set the softened tortilla on your work surface; spoon ⅓ cup of the pork filling over the bottom third of the circle; spread the filling flat and then fold the circle over the pork to cover it. Fold in the right and left circle sides and finish rolling up the tortilla. Secure with a toothpick and set it aside. Repeat the steaming and rolling to get a total of 8 pork rolls.

Pour enough oil into a skillet to make a depth of about 1 inch. Heat over medium-high heat until hot enough to pop a drop of flicked-in water. Fry the pork rolls, 2 at a time, on both sides, until they are golden amber. Lower the heat if the oil begins to smoke. Drain all the rolls on paper towels. Remove the toothpicks and let the rolls cool to room temperature. Transfer to a plastic bag; label with this page number and freeze.

To Cook

Preheat the oven to 425 degrees. Allow 2 rolls for each serving. Place the frozen rolls an inch or two apart on a baking pan or short length of aluminum foil. Bake for 15 minutes and serve.

Freezer-to-Oven Chicken Sticks

Serves 4
Cooking Time: 12 minutes

1 cup all-purpose flour	Oil for frying
1 teaspoon baking powder	Shortening for frying
1 ½ tablespoons onion powder	
1 tablespoon paprika	4 small freezer bags or 8
2 teaspoons salt	sandwich bags
¼ teaspoon pepper	
8 chicken thighs (about 3	
pounds total weight)	

In a mixing bowl, combine until well distributed the flour, baking powder, onion powder, paprika, salt, and pepper; set the bowl aside. Remove the skin and bones from the chicken thighs. Cut the chicken into long, uniform strips ¾ to 1 inch wide; put the strips in a bowl of cool water and set it aside.

Put approximately equal amounts of oil and shortening in a frying skillet to make a depth of ½ to ¾ inch. Heat over medium-high heat until very hot; stand back and flick a drop of water into the hot oil; when it makes a popping sound, you are ready to fry the strips. One at a time, coat the dripping chicken strips heavily in the dry ingredients and immediately place them in the hot oil; 4 thighs will fill a 10-inch pan, so you will probably have to do the frying in 2 batches. Once all the coated strips are in the oil, simmer them, uncovered, over medium-high heat for 5 minutes; carefully turn each soft-crusted piece; cover the skillet and simmer for 2 minutes. Then uncover the skillet and simmer for 2 more minutes. Remove the golden strips and drain them on paper towels.

When all the fried strips are completely cool, transfer them to a pan; cover with aluminum foil and freeze until solid. Divide the strips among 4 small freezer bags or doubled sandwich bags; each bag will contain 1 serving. Label the bags with this page number and return them to the freezer.

To Cook

Preheat the oven to 425 degrees. Allow 1 bag of strips for each portion. Place the frozen strips on an ungreased pan (or a larger baking sheet for multiple portions) at least ½ inch apart. Bake for 12 minutes and then serve.

Freezer-to-Oven Macedonian Meat Patties

Serves 4
Cooking Time: 10 minutes

4 slices bread
1 cup water
1 large egg
1 tablespoon minced fresh
    parsley leaves, or 1 teaspoon
    dried parsley flakes
1 teaspoon crushed dried mint
    leaves
½ teaspoon salt
1 small onion, finely chopped
1 pound ground beef

¾ cup all-purpose flour
¼ cup fine dry bread crumbs
¼ teaspoon pepper
Olive oil or cooking oil for
    frying
Your choice of a side dish from
    Chapter 11 (pages 211–21)

4 small freezer bags or
    8 sandwich bags

Remove the crusts from the bread; put the crustless bread in a
medium-size mixing bowl and add the water; when the water is
soaked into the bread, drain away all the excess water. Use your
hands to gently squeeze out more water to get a moist, dough-like
ball. Add the egg, parsley, mint, salt, and onion; blend the mixture
with your hands or a fork so that it is no longer lumpy; mix in the
ground beef and set it aside.

In another medium-size mixing bowl, combine the flour, bread
crumbs, and pepper; sprinkle some of this coating mixture over a
large cutting board or a baking sheet; set it aside. Pinch off chunks
of the meat mixture and roll them into balls about 1½ inches in
diameter. One at a time, generously dredge the balls in the bowl of
dry coating mixture; press each ball completely flat into a round, 2-
inch-wide patty that's about ¼ inch thick; press the coating mixture
into the meat as you flatten it, so that all the meat is coated. Place
the coated patties on the coating-dusted board or baking sheet.
Sprinkle any remaining coating mixture on top of the patties; let
them stand to absorb their coating for 10 minutes.

Pour oil to a depth of ½ inch into a large skillet. Heat over
medium-high to high heat until very hot and a drop of water flicked
into the oil pops. Fry the patties, half at a time, for about 7 minutes,
or until they are crusty brown on one side; then turn them over and
finish frying for about 3 more minutes. Drain on paper towels. Re-

peat for the other half of the patties. Allow the cooked patties to cool completely; then transfer them to a pan, cover loosely with aluminum foil or plastic wrap, and freeze for several hours, or until solid. Once frozen, divide the patties among 4 small freezer bags or doubled sandwich bags; each bag will contain 1 serving. Label the bags with this page number and return them to the freezer.

Prepare a side dish from Chapter 11 to accompany the meat patties; refrigerate it until ready to use.

To Cook

Preheat the oven to 425 degrees. Allow 1 bag of patties for each portion. Place the frozen patties on an ungreased pan (or a larger baking sheet for multiple portions) at least ½ inch apart. Bake for 10 minutes and serve with the side dish.

Freezer-to-Oven Fresh Salmon Cakes with Mushrooms and Dill

Serves 4
Cooking Time: 16 to 20 minutes

Here's a way to turn 2 fresh salmon steak portions into 4 servings of moist, delicately-flavored salmon cakes.

1 onion, coarsely chopped
2 celery stalks, scraped and coarsely chopped
1 carrot, coarsely chopped
4 whole black peppercorns, smashed slightly
2 cups water
½ lemon
1 pound fresh salmon, about 2 steak portions
10 tablespoons (1¼ sticks) butter
1 cup finely chopped onion

½ cup finely chopped fresh mushrooms
1 teaspoon salt
⅛ teaspoon pepper
3 tablespoons snipped fresh dillweed, or 2 teaspoons dried dill
Strained juice of 1 lemon
2 large eggs
10 small (2- by 2-inch squares) saltine crackers
Sour cream, optional
Lemon juice, optional

In a 2-quart pot, combine the coarsely chopped onion, celery, carrot, peppercorns, and water. Cut 2 thin slices off the lemon half and add them to the pot; then squeeze in the juice from the remainder of the lemon half. Bring the contents of the pot to a boil over high heat and add the salmon. Lower the heat and simmer for 5 to 8 minutes, or until the fish just flakes. Use a slotted spoon to remove the salmon to a plate and let it cool; discard the cooking water and vegetables. When cool enough to handle, remove all the skin and bones from the salmon. Shred the meat with your fingertips, but don't shred it into mush. Put the salmon (there will be 2 to 2½ cups) into a large mixing bowl and set it aside.

In a skillet, melt 4 tablespoons of the butter over medium to medium-high heat and sauté the finely chopped onion and mushrooms for a few minutes until they are limp; remove the skillet from the heat and stir in the salt, pepper, and dill. Mix the entire contents of the skillet into the salmon along with the strained lemon juice.

In a smaller bowl, beat the eggs until frothy; then set them aside. Put the saltines in a blender or crush them with a rolling pin to get cracker meal; stir the cracker meal into the eggs and let soak for 3 minutes. While you're waiting, lightly moisten the bottom of a 10-by 15-inch baking sheet with a small amount of water; cover with a layer of plastic wrap (the water makes it stick without wrinkling); set the baking sheet aside.

Scrape the cracker meal mixture into the salmon and blend with a fork. Form the mixture into a ball; put it on your work surface and divide it into 8 equal portions. Shape each portion into a flattened cake 3 to 3½ inches in diameter. Use a wide spatula to transfer the salmon cakes to the baking sheet. Cover the baking sheet with plastic wrap and put it in the freezer until the cakes are solid. Stack the frozen cakes with a length of plastic wrap between each one; put the stack in a freezer or bread bag; label with this page number and return to the freezer.

To Cook an Individual Serving

Melt 1½ tablespoons of butter in a small skillet over medium heat. When the butter bubbles, add 2 frozen salmon cakes and sauté for 8 to 10 minutes on one side; turn very carefully using 2 spatulas and sauté for 8 to 10 minutes on the other side, or until browned around the edges. Serve plain or with a dollop of cold sour cream or sprinkled with fresh lemon juice.

To Cook Multiple Servings

Cook following the directions above, using 1½ tablespoons of butter for every 2 cakes; reduce the butter to just 1 tablespoon for each 2-cake serving when cooking 3 portions together. Turn the cakes carefully in a crowded skillet.

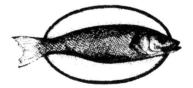

Freezer-to-Oven Batter-Dipped Fish Sticks

Serves 4
Cooking Time: 10 minutes

1¾ cups all-purpose flour
½ teaspoon onion powder
½ teaspoon salt
¾ cup lukewarm water
3 tablespoons olive oil
1 pound ¼-inch-thick fish
  fillets, such as flounder, sole,
  perch, or cod

Pepper or dried dill for
  sprinkling
1 large egg white
2 or 3 cups oil for frying

4 small freezer bags or 8
  sandwich bags

Whisk 1 cup of the flour, onion powder, and salt in a mixing bowl until blended. Combine the water and olive oil in a smaller bowl; whisk to blend and then gently blend the mixture into the flour to make a smooth cream; once it is lump-free, stop mixing. Cover the batter and set it aside for 2 hours before using.

When the batter is ready, cut the fish fillets into somewhat uniform strips about ¾ to 1 inch wide and 3 or 4 inches long. Plop the strips, several at a time, into a bowl containing the remaining ¾ cup flour; coat them on all sides and shake off the excess flour. Set the floured strips on a dinner plate and sprinkle them lightly with your choice of either pepper or dried dill; set aside.

Beat the egg white until medium-stiff but not dry peaks form; use a rubber spatula to gently fold it into the bowl of batter; set it aside.

Pour oil to a depth of ¾ inch into a skillet. Heat over medium-high to high heat until very hot and a drop of water flicked (at a distance) into the oil pops. Dip a floured strip of fish into the batter so that it is generously coated; then immediately slip it into the hot oil. Fry 6 to 8 strips at a time on both sides until golden amber. Drain on paper towels; sprinkle with salt if you like. Repeat frying all the fish sticks, adjusting the heat when necessary. Let the fried fish sticks cool.

Transfer the cooled fish sticks to a baking sheet; cover with plastic wrap and freeze until solid. Divide the sticks equally among 4 freezer bags or doubled sandwich bags; each bag will contain 1 serving. Label with this page number and return to the freezer.

To Cook

Preheat the oven to 425 degrees. Allow 1 bag for each portion. Place the frozen fish sticks on an ungreased baking pan or sheet at least ½ inch apart. Bake for 10 minutes and then serve.

Freezer-to-Oven Spinach and Feta Fillo Triangles

Makes about 30; or 7 to 10 servings
Cooking Time: 15 minutes

1 8-ounce box frozen Apollo Fillo, or half a 16-ounce box Athens Fillo Strudel Leaves	½ teaspoon salt
	½ teaspoon dried dill
	6 tablespoons (¾ stick) butter
1 pound fresh spinach	6 tablespoons shortening
4 ounces feta cheese	
1 large egg, lightly beaten	2 aluminum foil freezer pans

Allow the box of fillo to thaw in your refrigerator either overnight or for 8 hours; then let it stand at room temperature for at least 1½ hours before using. If you try to rush the thawing or attempt to work with cold fillo, it will only prove to be unmanageable.

Prepare the filling by first putting the spinach leaves into a kitchen sink full of cool water; rinse well to remove all grit. Remove and discard the stems from the spinach leaves; spread the leaves over many generous layers of paper towels to absorb all the excess moisture. When all the leaves are stemless and on paper towels, cover them with more paper towels and snugly roll up the whole lot of them, jelly roll fashion, so that absolutely no water remains in the leaves. (The reason for all this fuss is to prevent the spinach from sogging up at the bottom of each triangle later on.) Unroll the dry spinach leaves; stack 3 or 4 on top of each other; snugly roll up like a cigar and use a sharp knife to shred the leaves as thinly and finely as you can. Put the shredded spinach in a large mixing bowl; shred all the spinach in this manner. Crumble the feta cheese with your fingers into small bits and mix it into the spinach. Then mix in the egg, salt, and dill. Set the filling aside.

In a small saucepan, heat the butter and shortening. Once melted, set the butter mixture over the lowest possible heat to keep it melted but not browned. Brush 2 large rimmed baking pans with a heavy film of melted butter; set them aside to solidify.

To make the triangles, have in front of you the spinach filling, the melted butter, and the box of fillo. Spread the fillo out flat in front of you so that the shorter side of the rectangle faces you; cut the fillo down the center from top to bottom to get 2 long rectangular strips. Cover the strips with a very slightly dampened, non-terrycloth towel. (If you are using the 16-ounce box of 18- by 14-inch fillo, cut it in half to get 2 rectangles that are 9 by 14 inches. Wrap and re-freeze 1 rectangle. Turn the other rectangle, shorter side facing you, and cut it into the 2 rectangular strips described above.) Uncover and place one of the rectangle strips on your work surface, short side facing you. Brush the top sheet generously with some melted butter leaving a ¼-inch margin all around.

Place a heaping teaspoon of filling 3 inches above the short side facing you and just a little bit to the left. Bring the bottom right corner point of just the one buttered sheet of fillo up and over the filling, so that it covers the filling and meets flush with the left side of the strip. Now that the triangle has been established, fold the bottom point straight up to meet flush left bringing the whole triangle with it. Fold the bottom left point toward the right to meet flush right, again bringing the whole triangle with it. Continue folding twice more (it is a lot like folding up a flag) until the triangle is complete. Place the triangle, seam side down, on the buttered baking sheet. Repeat this process for all the filling and fillo. Make sure to work quickly as fillo dries and crumbles with time.

Brush the 2 baking pans full of completed triangles generously with the remaining butter. Place the pans, uncovered, in the freezer for several hours, or until the triangles are solid. Gently transfer them to 2 aluminum foil freezer pans, being careful not to break off the tips of the triangles. Cover; label with this page number and return to the freezer.

To Cook

Preheat the oven to 425 degrees. Allow 3 or 4 frozen triangles for each serving. Place them, at least ½ inch apart, on a rimmed baking pan. Bake for 15 minutes, or until golden.

To Cook the Triangles Before Freezing

Place the just-made triangles on a lightly buttered baking pan. Bake at 350 degrees for 15 minutes, or until golden. Once baked, do not freeze.

OTHER FREEZER-TO-OVEN RECIPES
FROM THIS BOOK

Chicken Cutlets with Basil and Tomato

Prepare this variation of the Chicken Cutlets in Fresh Herbs and Wine recipe (page 82) using chicken that has never been frozen before. Package the raw, marinated cutlets between their lengths of plastic wrap in a freezer bag and freeze, flat, until solid. Label with this page number.

To Cook an Individual Serving

Heat 1½ tablespoons of butter in a large skillet over medium to medium-high heat. When the sizzling subsides, add 3 frozen cutlets without overlapping them. Sauté the cutlets, untouched, for about 2 minutes; when they are white at the edges and limp, swirl them gently around the skillet. When the cutlets' centers begin to whiten, turn them over and continue sautéing for 2 more minutes, or until they are hot at the center; don't overcook them.

Multiple servings are cooked in the same manner.

Quebec Tourtières

Prepare these meat pies (page 195), using either fresh or previously-frozen ground pork; fry and cool as directed. Freeze on a baking sheet; then transfer the pies to a plastic bag, label with this page number, and return to the freezer.

To Cook

Preheat the oven to 425 degrees. Allow 4 frozen pies for each serving. Place them on an ungreased baking sheet or length of aluminum foil. Bake for 12 minutes.

Tidy Tacos

Prepare the tacos (page 199), using either fresh or previously-frozen meat; bake and cool as directed. Package the tacos in a plastic bag, label with this page number, and freeze.

To Cook

Preheat the oven to 425 degrees. Allow 2 frozen tacos for each serving. Place them on their sides in a rimmed baking pan. Bake for 15 minutes.

Beef and Cheddar Fillo Sticks

Prepare the fillo sticks (page 200), using either fresh or previously-frozen ground beef. After rolling up and buttering the complete pan of unbaked fillo sticks, refrigerate them to solidify the butter. Carefully transfer the fillo sticks, side-by-side but not touching and seam side down, to a freezer pan; cover and freeze.

To Cook

Preheat the oven to 425 degrees. Allow 2 frozen fillo sticks for each serving. Place them, several inches apart, in a baking pan or on a baking sheet. Bake for 20 minutes.

Fondue Slices

Prepare the recipe (page 206), refrigerating the pan of uncooked, soaking bread slices overnight. Lift each slice carefully out of the pan with a dinner knife and place it, sauce side up, on a baking sheet. Spread any remaining sauce from the emptied pan back onto the bread slices. Place the baking sheet of slices, uncovered, in the freezer until solid. Transfer the solid slices to a plastic bag or wrap in aluminum foil, label with this page number, and return to the freezer.

To Cook

Preheat the oven to 450 degrees. Place 2 frozen slices for each serving, sauce side up, on a baking sheet or length of aluminum foil. Bake for 15 minutes, or until bubbly at the center.

❦ 4 ❧

MARINATED MEALS

The dinner meats for these meals acquire their flavor by marinating for one or several days. They await a quick cooking, usually broiling, minutes before serving time.

Beef Kabobs in Red Wine and Herbs

Beef Teriyaki

Spicy-Hot, Orange Beef Kabobs

Pounded Pork Chops, Three Ways

Shish Kabob

Quick-Broil Curried Lamb Shanks

Dilled Fish Fillets

Chicken Cutlets in Fresh Herbs and Wine

Quick-Broil Barbecued Chicken

Quick Chick-Teri

Beef Kabobs in Red Wine and Herbs

Serves 4
Cooking Time: 7 to 15 minutes

2 pounds boneless, lean, thick
  beef, such as London broil
  or beef kabob cubes
½ cup dry red wine
3 tablespoons fresh lemon
  juice
1 tablespoon olive oil
1 tablespoon corn oil

2 garlic cloves
½ teaspoon dried oregano
½ teaspoon salt
½ teaspoon pepper
Rice Pilaf (page 213)

4 10- to 12-inch-long bamboo
  or metal skewers

Trim any excess fat from the meat; then cut the meat into uniform
1¼-inch cubes. Count the number of cubes; divide that number by
4 and make a small written note of the number. Put the meat cubes
in a small-to-medium-size mixing bowl; tape the noted number to
the outside of the bowl and set the bowl aside.

Make the marinade by combining the next 8 ingredients (through
the pepper). Pour the marinade over the meat and mix it in gently
with your fingers; cover the surface of the meat directly with plastic
wrap. Let the meat marinate at room temperature for 1 to 3 hours.
(Use your own judgment on this: If the temperature is over 80
degrees, then refrigerate the meat until you are ready to use it—for
up to 2 days.)

Prepare the Rice Pilaf and refrigerate it until needed.

To Cook an Individual Serving

Prepare 1 portion of the Rice Pilaf following the directions on
page 214.

Preheat the oven to broil; set the rack closest to the heat source.
If you are using an electric oven, keep the oven door slightly ajar
now and during the broiling time. The number taped to the bowl is
the number of beef cubes to be used for each portion; thread the
appropriate number onto a skewer and place the skewer in a shallow
pan.

Broil the meat on the top rack, turning once at the halfway point,
approximately 7 to 9 minutes for rare, 9 to 12 minutes for medium-

rare, or 12 to 15 minutes for well-done. Slash a cube with a knife to test for the desired doneness. Serve, unskewered, over a bed of hot pilaf.

To Cook Multiple Servings

Cook following the directions above, multiplying the skewer and pilaf portions accordingly.

Beef Teriyaki

Serves 4
Cooking Time: 7 to 15 minutes

2 pounds boneless, lean, thick
   beef, such as London broil
   or beef kabob cubes
½ cup soy sauce
¼ cup fresh lime or lemon
   juice
2 tablespoons sugar
2 tablespoons corn oil

2 large garlic cloves, smashed
   and very finely minced
½ teaspoon ground ginger
Rice Pilaf (page 213), using
   beef broth

4 10- to 12-inch-long bamboo
   or metal skewers

Trim any excess fat from the meat; then cut the meat into uniform 1¼-inch cubes. Count the number of cubes; divide that number by 4; make a small written note of the number. Put the meat cubes in a small-to-medium size mixing bowl; tape the noted number to the outside of the bowl and set the bowl aside.

Make the marinade by stirring together the soy sauce, lime juice, and sugar; when the sugar has dissolved, blend in the oil, garlic, and ginger. Pour the marinade over the meat and mix it in gently with your fingers; cover the surface of the meat directly with plastic wrap. Let the meat marinate at room temperature for 1 to 3 hours. (Use your own judgment on this: If the temperature is over 80 degrees, then refrigerate the meat until you are ready to use it—for up to 2 days.)

Prepare the Rice Pilaf, substituting regular-strength beef broth plus 1 teaspoon of soy sauce for the chicken broth; refrigerate until needed.

To Cook an Individual Serving

Prepare 1 portion of the Rice Pilaf following the directions on page 214.

Preheat the oven to broil; set the rack closest to the heat source. If you are using an electric oven, keep the oven door slightly ajar now and during the broiling time. The number taped to the bowl is the number of beef cubes to be used for each portion; thread the appropriate number onto a skewer and place the skewer in a shallow pan.

Broil the meat on the top rack, turning once at the halfway point, approximately 7 to 9 minutes for rare, 9 to 12 minutes for medium-rare, or 12 to 15 minutes for well-done. Slash a cube with a knife to test for the desired doneness. Serve, unskewered, over a bed of hot pilaf.

To Cook Multiple Servings

Cook following the directions above, multiplying the skewer and pilaf portions accordingly.

Variation:

STEAK TERIYAKI

Cut about 2 pounds of moderately-priced-to-inexpensive steak (bone removed, if necessary) into 4 equal portions; place the pieces snugly but in a single layer in a glass or ceramic baking dish. Prepare the above marinade and pour it over the steaks. Turn each steak once; cover and marinate as directed, turning the steaks over from time to time. Broil each portion to the desired doneness.

Spicy-Hot, Orange Beef Kabobs

Serves 4
Cooking Time: 7 to 15 minutes

2 tablespoons orange extract
3 tablespoons corn oil
2 oranges
2 pounds boneless, lean, thick
   beef, such as London broil
   or beef kabob cubes
1/3 cup frozen orange juice
   concentrate, thawed
3 tablespoons soy sauce
2 tablespoons fresh lemon
   juice

2 1/2 teaspoons Tabasco sauce,
   or up to 1 teaspoon more to
   taste
1/2 teaspoon ground ginger
1/2 teaspoon celery seed,
   ground in a mortar and
   pestle
1/2 teaspoon salt
Ramen Noodles (page 215)

4 10- to 12-inch-long bamboo
   or metal skewers

The night before you prepare this recipe, measure the orange extract into a custard cup or small shallow bowl; leave it, uncovered, overnight. The next day, all the alcohol and water will have evaporated leaving nothing but a film of a residue of orange oil; stir the corn oil into this. Using the coarse side of a cheese grater, scrape the rinds off the oranges to get 2 tablespoons of grated rind (don't scrape too deeply into the white, bitter part of the orange's skin). Mix the grated rind into the custard cup of orange-and-corn oil and set it aside for at least 15 minutes. Wrap and save the oranges for some other use.

Trim any excess fat from the meat; then cut the meat into uniform 1 1/4-inch cubes. Count the number of cubes; divide that number by 4 and make a small written note of the number. Put the meat cubes in a small-to-medium-size mixing bowl; tape the noted number to the outside of the bowl and set the bowl aside.

Make the marinade by combining the orange juice concentrate, soy sauce, lemon juice, Tabasco sauce, ginger, celery seed, and salt; blend in the oil and rind mixture from the custard cup. Note that the marinade is for a medium-hot taste; you can increase the Tabasco sauce if you prefer more heat. Pour the marinade over the meat and mix it in gently with your fingers; cover the surface of the meat directly with plastic wrap. Let the meat marinate at room temperature for 1 to 3 hours. (Use your own judgment on this: If the temperature is over 80 degrees, then refrigerate the meat until you are ready to use it—for up to 2 days.)

To Cook an Individual Serving

Prepare 1 portion of Ramen Noodles following the directions on page 215. Preheat the oven to broil; set the rack closest to the heat source. If you are using an electric oven, keep the oven door slightly ajar now and during the broiling time. The number taped to the bowl is the number of beef cubes to be used for each portion; thread the appropriate number onto a skewer and place in a shallow pan.

Broil the meat on the top rack, turning once at the halfway point, approximately 7 to 9 minutes for rare, 9 to 12 minutes for medium-rare, or 12 to 15 minutes for well-done. Slash a cube with a knife to test for the desired doneness. Serve, unskewered, alongside the ramen noodles.

To Cook Multiple Servings

Cook following the directions above, multiplying the skewer and ramen noodle portions accordingly.

Pounded Pork Chops, Three Ways

Serves 4
Cooking Time: 6 minutes

These pork chops are pounded to make them especially tender; then they are covered with your choice of marinade. The flavorful results can be cooked in 6 minutes.

8 small-to-medium pork chops, about ½ to ¾ inch thick	4 tablespoons butter
Your choice of marinade (recipes follow)	Plastic wrap

Make the pounded pork chops: Trim off all excess fat around each chop's outer rim. Place pork chop #1 in the center of a 12-inch square of plastic wrap; cover it with a double-ply, 12-inch square of plastic wrap. Put this package, double-ply-up, on the floor; use a wooden or rubber mallet to pound the chop as thinly as possible without tearing the meat; pound right up to the bone; do not unwrap the plastic wrap. (The rubber mallets from auto-supply stores are lots cheaper than the wooden kind and are dishwasher-safe. Lacking either kind of mallet, use a heavy cast-iron skillet or a flat-sided rock.) Repeat the pounding in this manner using new plastic wrap for each chop.

Remove the top layer of plastic wrap from pork chop #1; spread it out smoothly on your work surface. Spread the correct amount of marinade over one side of the now-exposed chop; turn the chop, marinade side down, onto the smoothed-out plastic wrap; spread the correct amount of marinade over the plain side of the chop; cover with its plastic wrap and place on a dinner plate. Repeat this procedure for all the chops. Refrigerate the plate of chops until ready to use—for up to 1½ days.

To Cook an Individual Serving

In a large frying pan over medium heat, melt 1 tablespoon of the butter. When it bubbles, add 2 of the unwrapped chops. Cook for 3 minutes on each side, or until no more rosiness remains even at the bones; maintain the heat at no more than medium to ensure tenderness; don't overcook. Serve at once.

To Cook Multiple Servings

Cook the chops, 2 for each serving and 2 at a time, since even a large frying pan can accommodate no more than that. Replenish the butter, 1 tablespoon for every 2 chops, between cookings as necessary.

Mexican Chili Chops Marinade

3 tablespoons corn oil
1 tablespoon chili powder
½ teaspoon ground cumin

4 tablespoons grated onion
2 small garlic cloves, smashed
 and very finely minced

Combine the oil and spices; then stir in the garlic and onion. Let the marinade stand for 15 minutes before using. Use ½ teaspoon marinade for each side of a chop (i.e., 1 teaspoon for each whole chop).

Pork Chops in Mustard Marinade

3 tablespoons either Dijon or
 spicy brown mustard, such
 as Kosciusko or Gulden's

3 tablespoons corn oil
2 tablespoons grated onion

Vigorously stir the ingredients together until completely blended. Use 1 level teaspoon of marinade for each side of a chop (i.e., 2 level teaspoons for each whole chop).

Pork Chops Piccante Marinade

3 tablespoons corn oil
3 tablespoons grated lemon
rind (from the coarse side of
a cheese grater)
1 ½ teaspoons fresh lemon
juice

½ teaspoon dried oregano,
crushed between the heels of
your hands
¼ teaspoon pepper

Combine all the ingredients until smooth. Let the marinade stand
for 15 minutes before using. Use 1 level teaspoon of marinade for
each side of a chop (i.e., 2 level teaspoons for each whole chop).

Shish Kabob

Serves 4
Cooking Time: 6 to 14 minutes

1 half-leg of lamb (about 3 pounds), either the shank or sirloin half
½ cup fresh lemon juice
¼ cup olive oil
¼ cup corn oil
1 garlic clove, smashed and very finely minced

1 tablespoon dried oregano, crushed between the heels of your hands
¼ teaspoon pepper
Rice Pilaf (page 213)

4 10- to 12-inch-long bamboo or metal skewers

Trim the excess fat from the lamb; then cut big hunks of meat off the bone and cut the meat into 1¼-inch cubes or chunks. Put the lamb cubes in a small-to-medium-size mixing bowl and set the bowl aside.

Make the marinade by combining the lemon juice, olive and corn oils, garlic, oregano, and pepper; blend until smooth. Pour the marinade over the lamb and mix it in gently with your fingers; cover the surface of the meat directly with plastic wrap. Let the meat marinate at room temperature for 1 to 3 hours. (Use your own judgment on this: If the temperature is over 80 degrees, then refrigerate the meat until you are ready to use it—for up to 2 days.)

Prepare the Rice Pilaf and refrigerate it until needed.

To Cook an Individual Serving

Prepare 1 portion of the Rice Pilaf following the directions on page 214.

Preheat the oven to broil; set the rack closest to the heat source. If you are using an electric oven, keep the oven door ajar now and during the broiling time. Thread one fourth of the lamb cubes (they will probably vary in size) onto a skewer; place the skewer in a shallow pan.

Broil the shish kabob on the top rack turning once at the halfway point for approximately 6 to 8 minutes for rare, 8 to 10 minutes for medium-rare, or 10 to 14 minutes for well-done. Slash one of the bigger pieces of lamb to test for the desired doneness. Serve, unskewered, over a hot bed of pilaf.

To Cook Multiple Servings

Cook following the directions above, multiplying the skewer and pilaf portions accordingly.

Quick-Broil Curried Lamb Shanks

Serves 4
Cooking Time: 15 minutes

Presteaming the lamb shanks both tenderizes them and removes their excess fat. They await a quick cooking while steeping in a flavorful curry marinade. Serve with a side dish from Chapter 11.

3 tablespoons butter
4 lamb shanks (about 3 to 4 pounds total weight)
1 medium-size onion, chopped
4 whole black peppercorns
2 tablespoons curry powder
¼ cup strained fresh lemon juice

2 tablespoons corn oil
2 tablespoons honey

2 quart-size, zip-lock plastic food storage bags (7 by 8 inches)

Melt 1 tablespoon of the butter in a medium-size skillet over medium-high heat. When it browns, sear 2 of the lamb shanks on all sides until browned; place in a pot that will accommodate all 4 shanks in a single layer. Melt another tablespoon of the butter in the skillet and sear the remaining 2 shanks; then add them to the pot. Melt the last tablespoon of butter in the skillet, lower the heat to medium, and sauté the onion until it is limp but not brown; scrape the onion into the pot with the lamb shanks. Add the peppercorns.

Once the shanks are in a single layer in their cooking pot, add water to a depth of ½ inch; bring to a boil, cover, and maintain a steady simmer for 45 minutes, turning the shanks over at the halfway point.

When cooked, transfer the shanks to a plate to cool, uncovered, while you make the curry marinade from the remaining ingredients. Strain and refrigerate the lamb broth for another use. Put 2 cool shanks in each plastic zip-lock bag; pour the marinade equally between each; seal snugly and then open up a corner and press out all the air trapped inside; reseal the bags and turn them over several times to distribute the marinade. Put the bags on 2 dinner plates and let stand at room temperature for 1 to 3 hours turning the bags over from time to time. (Use your own judgment on this: If the temperature is over 80 degrees, then refrigerate the meat until you are ready to use it—for up to 2 days.)

To Cook an Individual Serving

Preheat the oven to broil; set the rack at its second rung so that it is 6 inches from the heat source; if you are using an electric oven, keep the oven door slightly ajar now and during the broiling time. Place 1 lamb shank in a shallow pan and broil it for a total of 15 minutes, turning once at the halfway point.

To Cook Multiple Servings

Cook following the directions above, using 1 lamb shank for each serving.

Dilled Fish Fillets

Serves 4
Cooking Time: 5 to 10 minutes

1 to 1½ pounds boneless fish
  fillets
⅓ cup strained fresh lemon
  juice
3 tablespoons dry white wine,
  preferable but optional
3 tablespoons corn oil
1½ tablespoons snipped fresh
  dillweed, or ¾ teaspoon
  dried dill

2 tablespoons butter

2 quart-size, zip-lock plastic
  food storage bags (7 to 8
  inches)

Place the fish fillets in one layer in the 2 plastic bags, dividing the fillets so that there are 2 equal servings in each bag. Make the marinade by combining the lemon juice, wine, oil, and dill. Stir the marinade until it is smooth; then immediately pour it equally into both bags of fish; seal snugly and then open up a corner and press out all the air trapped inside; reseal the bags. Hold a bag across your upturned palm and slosh it around so that the dill works to both sides of the fish. Put both bags on a dinner plate and refrigerate for at least 2 hours before using, or for up to 1½ days.

To Cook an Individual Serving

Preheat the oven to broil; set the rack on the second rung so that it's 6 inches away from the heat source. If you are using an electric oven, keep the oven door slightly ajar now and during the broiling time. Using ½ tablespoon of butter per portion of fish, lightly grease the bottom of a shallow pan with some of this butter. Place half of the fish from one of the plastic bags (i.e.: one portion), skin side down, in the pan; dot with the butter remaining in the ½ tablespoon and drizzle with 1 tablespoon of the marinade.

Broil thin-to-medium fillets, without turning, for approximately 5 minutes, or until the fish flakes at the center; broil thicker fillets about 10 minutes, turning them over halfway, until flaky at the center.

Transfer the fish to a dinner plate; jiggle the cooking pan to mix the juices and pour them over the fish; then serve immediately.

To Cook Multiple Servings

Cook following the directions above, using ½ tablespoon of butter and 1 tablespoon of marinade for every half-bag portion of fish.

Chicken Cutlets in Fresh Herbs and Wine

Serves 4
Cooking Time: 2 to 4 minutes

6 chicken thighs	2 tablespoons olive oil
¼ cup snipped fresh parsley leaves	2 tablespoons corn oil
	¼ cup dry white wine
2 tablespoons snipped fresh rosemary leaves, or 2 teaspoons dried rosemary	4 tablespoons butter

Remove the skin and bones from the chicken pieces; cut each thigh into 2 equal pieces as you are removing the bone. Place each chicken piece between generous, doubled lengths of plastic wrap. Pound each piece with a mallet or the bottom of a flat heavy skillet until the meat is thin but not shredded. Set the cutlets aside.

In a blender, combine the remaining ingredients, except the butter, in the order listed; whirl at high speed until the mixture is smooth and bright green. Spread 1 teaspoon of this blended marinade on each side of each cutlet (i.e.: use 2 teaspoons for each whole cutlet). Rewrap each cutlet; place the whole lot on a dinner plate and refrigerate until ready to use—for up to 1 day.

To Cook an Individual Serving

In a large frying pan, melt 1 tablespoon of the butter over medium to medium-high heat. When it sizzles and bubbles, add 3 of the unwrapped cutlets. Cook for a minute or two on each side, or until no more pink remains; don't overcook. Serve at once.

To Cook Multiple Servings

Cook following the directions above, using 3 cutlets for each serving and 1 tablespoon of butter for each serving.

Variations:

CHICKEN CUTLETS IN FRESH HERBS WITHOUT WINE

Replace the wine in the above recipe with 2½ tablespoons of strained fresh lemon or lime juice. Increase the corn oil from 2 to 3 tablespoons.

CHICKEN CUTLETS WITH BASIL AND TOMATO

Replace the blender mixture with a hand-mixed combination of 4 tablespoons of tomato paste and 2 tablespoons of dried basil (or ⅓ cup snipped fresh basil leaves). Rub ½ teaspoon of this marinade over each side of each cutlet (i.e.: use 1 teaspoon for each cutlet). Rewrap, refrigerate, and cook as directed above. A side dish of buttered spaghetti complements this well.

Quick-Broil Barbecued Chicken

Serves 4
Cooking Time: 14 minutes

This 15-minute dinner offers tender chicken pieces coated in a hearty barbecue glaze plus barbecue flavor right down to the bone.

1 chicken, quartered, or 4 chicken legs or 4 chicken breast halves, according to preference	1 cup bottled barbecue sauce ⅓ cup water

Place the chicken pieces, skin side down and in a single layer, in an accommodating, non-aluminum cooking pot. Combine ⅔ cup of the barbecue sauce with the ⅓ cup of water and stir to blend; then pour the mixture over the chicken. Cover the pot and bring to a boil over medium-high heat; then lower the heat and maintain a steady simmer for 30 minutes, turning the pieces over at the halfway point.

Transfer the chicken pieces to a dinner plate and let them cool, uncovered. Simmer the barbecue sauce in the pot, uncovered, over medium-high heat for 8 to 10 minutes, stirring from time to time at first and then, later, constantly, until it is reduced to the thickness of the original barbecue sauce before the water was added to it. Remove the pot from the heat and return the chicken pieces to the pot, skin side down and in a single layer. Brush the upturned sides of the chicken pieces with the remaining ⅓ cup of bottled barbecue sauce. Cover the pot and refrigerate until ready to use—for up to 2 days.

To Cook an Individual Serving

Preheat the oven to broil; set the rack on the second rung so that it is 6 inches away from the heat source. If you are using an electric oven, keep the oven door slightly ajar now and during the broiling time.

Put 1 chicken quarter, skin side down, in a shallow pan; baste it with some of the barbecue sauce from the cooking pot. Broil for 7 minutes; then turn the piece over, baste the skin with some more sauce, and broil for 7 more minutes. Serve.

To Cook Multiple Servings

Cook following the directions above, using 1 chicken quarter for each serving.

Quick Chick-Teri

Serves 4
Cooking Time: 14 minutes

1 chicken, quartered, or 4 chicken legs or 4 chicken breast halves, according to preference	3 tablespoons light brown sugar
3 tablespoons corn oil	½ teaspoon ground ginger
1 garlic clove, smashed and minced	½ cup soy sauce
	1 tablespoon cornstarch
	1 tablespoon cold water

Put the chicken pieces, skin side down and in a single layer, in a non-aluminum, accommodating cooking pot; set it aside. In a small saucepan, heat the oil over medium heat. Add the garlic and sauté until it just begins to turn amber; then remove the pan from the heat. Strain the oil into a small heatproof mixing bowl and discard the garlic. Stir the sugar and ginger into the oil; then add the soy sauce and pour the mixture over the chicken. Cover the pot and bring to a boil over medium-high heat; then lower the heat and maintain a steady simmer for 30 minutes, turning the chicken pieces over at the halfway point.

Transfer the chicken pieces to a dinner plate and let them cool, uncovered. Combine the cornstarch and water in a small cup; set it aside. Bring the pot of sauce to a steady simmer over medium heat. Re-mix the cornstarch and immediately stir it into the sauce; stir constantly and lower the heat to a simmer. Stir and simmer until the sauce is bubbly and thickened. Remove the pot from the heat; spoon out 5 tablespoons of the thickened sauce to a heatproof cup and set aside. Return the chicken pieces to the pot, skin side down and in a single layer; spoon the reserved sauce evenly over the upturned sides of the chicken pieces. Let the sauce and chicken cool to room temperature; then cover and refrigerate until ready to use—for up to 2 days.

To Cook an Individual Serving

Preheat the oven to broil; set the rack on the second rung so that it is 6 inches away from the heat source. If you are using an electric oven, keep the oven door ajar now and during the broiling time.

Put 1 chicken quarter, skin side down, in a shallow pan; spread some of the solidified sauce over it. Broil for 7 minutes; turn the piece over, spread the skin with more sauce, and broil for 7 more minutes. Serve.

To Cook Multiple Servings

Cook following the directions above, using 1 chicken quarter for each serving.

❧ 5 ❧

COMPONENT DINNERS

Here are some dinners that have two to three separate component parts. The components are made ahead and refrigerated until you are ready to quickly assemble and cook them.

Instant Roast Beef Stew

Taco Salad with Hot Shredded Steak

Unstuffed Cabbage

Chicken and Artichoke Hearts in Velvet Avgolemono

Tender Chicken Cutlets in Fresh Mushroom Sauce

Green Bean and Bacon Soup

Pork Cutlets in Spiced Salsa

Two-Minute Fish Fillets in Shrimp Sauce

Ready-to-Pour Quiches with Ham and Cheese

Instant Roast Beef Stew

Serves 4
Cooking Time: 5 to 7 minutes

Here's a classic beef stew ready for instant serving. The meat remains as tender as roast beef and the vegetables retain their just-cooked flavor. The secret is in the quick assembly of components and the use of a roasting beef instead of stew meat. Any high-to-medium quality, boneless oven roast will work as long as it's not one used for pot roast. Since roast beef is rarely sold in 2-pound portions, you may want to buy a 4- to 4½-pound roast and halve it; freeze the other half to repeat this recipe later.

1 2- to 2¼-pound boneless, oven-ready roast beef
2 13¾-ounce cans regular-strength beef broth
4 tablespoons butter
1 cup chopped onion
1¼ cups peeled carrots sliced into ¼-inch rounds
3 cups peeled potatoes cut into ¾-inch dice
Salt and pepper to taste
6 tablespoons all-purpose flour
⅔ cup dry red wine, or ⅔ cup beef broth mixed with 1 tablespoon Worcestershire sauce

Let the roast beef stand at room temperature for 1 to 2 hours. Preheat the oven to 325 degrees. Put the meat, fat side up, in a baking pan and roast for 40 to 45 minutes (i.e.: 20 minutes per pound), or until the meat is on the rare side of medium-rare. (Even if you usually prefer your meat more done, keep it rare-ish now, since it will continue cooking after it is removed from the oven and it will later be heated with the stew ingredients.) Remove the roast from the oven, put it on a dinner plate, and let it cool, uncovered, to lukewarm. Pour 1 can of beef broth into the roasting pan, stir to loosen the drippings, and set the pan aside.

While the beef cooks and cools, continue with the following: Melt 2 tablespoons of the butter in a medium-to-large skillet over medium-high heat. When it sizzles, sauté the onion until soft; lower the heat to a simmer and spread the onion out in a layer to cover the skillet's bottom; simmer for 15 minutes, stirring now and then, until the onion becomes a slightly amber color. Remove the skillet from the heat and set it aside.

Pour the combined pan drippings and beef broth into a cooking pot and add the remaining can of beef broth. Bring to a boil and add the carrots and potatoes; then return to a boil, cover, and simmer gently for 10 to 12 minutes, or until the potatoes test just done. Turn off the heat and use a slotted spoon to immediately remove the vegetables to a dinner plate; sprinkle them with salt and pepper to taste; let them cool, uncovered. Cover the pot of broth. Trim the fat from the cooled beef. Cut the meat into uniform ½-inch dice; sprinkle it with salt and pepper and set it aside.

Over medium heat, melt the remaining 2 tablespoons of butter into the onion in the skillet. Remove the skillet from the heat and stir in the flour until it has been absorbed. Slowly stir in either the wine or the broth-Worcestershire mixture until no lumps remain; slowly stir in the beef broth until the mixture is smooth. Return the skillet to medium- to medium-high heat; stir until the mixture bubbles and thickens; remove from the heat. Let the stew sauce cool, uncovered, to room temperature; stir now and then to prevent a film from forming on the top.

Divide the diced cooled meat into 4 equal portions of about 1 cup each; put each portion in its own 2-cup plastic container and add equal amounts of the carrot-potato mixture. Cover each container and refrigerate until ready to use—for up to 2 days.

When the sauce is cool, pour it into a 3-cup container, cover, and refrigerate until ready to use.

To Cook an Individual Serving

Spoon ¾ cup of the stew sauce into a saucepan and set it over medium-high heat for a minute or two until liquid is bubbling. Gently stir in 1 container of meat and vegetables until they are coated. Let the stew come to a boil; then cover, lower the heat, and let it simmer for 3 to 4 minutes, or until heated through. Serve.

To Cook Multiple Servings

Cook following the directions above, multiplying the portions accordingly.

Taco Salad with Hot Shredded Steak

Serves 4
Cooking Time: about 5 minutes

1 ½ pounds boneless sirloin
   steak
⅓ cup corn oil
½ cup chopped onion
1 garlic clove, smashed and
   minced
4 ¼ teaspoons chili powder
¼ teaspoon plus ⅛ teaspoon
   ground cumin
1 teaspoon tomato paste
Salt to taste
Cayenne pepper to taste
2 tablespoons distilled white
   vinegar

¼ teaspoon salt
¼ cup bottled chili sauce
4 ounces sharp Cheddar
   cheese
1 teaspoon all-purpose flour
1 head iceberg lettuce
2 medium-size ripe tomatoes
½ cup chopped black olives,
   optional
¼ cup chopped scallions,
   optional
¾ cup sour cream, optional
2 cups plain nacho corn chips,
   broken into 1-inch pieces

Trim all the fat from the steak; then cut the meat into long strips, ½ inch wide. Use your sharpest knife to slice across the strips as thinly as possible to get thin, shred-like bits. Heat 1 tablespoon of the oil in a skillet over medium-high heat; add the onion and garlic and sauté until soft. Add the steak shreds and sauté until no pink remains. When the juices begin to flow, turn the heat to low and stir in 4 teaspoons of the chili powder, ¼ teaspoon of the ground cumin, the tomato paste, and salt and cayenne pepper to taste. Stir until the liquids thicken; then remove from the heat and allow to cool. Cover and refrigerate until ready to use—for up to 2 days.

Make the dressing by combining ¼ cup of the corn oil with the vinegar, ¼ teaspoon salt, ¼ teaspoon chili powder, and ⅛ teaspoon ground cumin; blend in the chili sauce; store, refrigerated, in a covered jar.

Shred the cheese to get 1 closely packed cup; mix in the flour to prevent stickiness; package and refrigerate until ready to use.

Rinse the lettuce and remove the core; let the excess water drain off. Cut the head into 4 equal quarters; wrap and refrigerate.

Cut the tomatoes into bite-size pieces and refrigerate in a covered container. Prepare the olives and scallions, if desired; refrigerate them in separate containers. Measure the sour cream into a container, sprinkle with salt to taste, and stir until smooth; cover and refrigerate.

To Cook an Individual Serving

Tear one of the lettuce quarters into an ample, individual-serving salad bowl; add ¼ cup of the shredded cheese, one fourth of the tomatoes, 2 tablespoons of chopped olives, and 1 tablespoon of scallions; toss. Add ½ cup of nacho chips and toss again. Drizzle 2 tablespoons of the dressing over the salad and set it aside without tossing.

Heat 1 tablespoon of water in a small skillet over high heat; add ½ cup of the shredded steak and use 2 spoons to stir the meat over high heat for 1 to 2 minutes, or until the water has evaporated. Pour the steak into the salad and toss well; top the salad with 2 heaping tablespoons of sour cream, if you wish. Serve immediately.

To Cook Multiple Servings

Prepare the combined salad portions in your largest salad or mixing bowl; then serve at the table in individual plates, topping each serving with sour cream. Multiply the portions accordingly; if you are cooking all 4 steak portions at once, reduce the water by 1 tablespoon.

Unstuffed Cabbage

Serves 4
Cooking Time: 20 minutes

1 pound lean ground beef
½ cup chopped onion
4 cups shredded and chopped raw cabbage
1 cup long-grain converted rice
1½ teaspoons crushed dried mint leaves
1½ teaspoons salt

¼ teaspoon pepper
1 6-ounce can tomato paste
½ cup fresh lemon juice
1½ cups water
1 15-ounce can tomato sauce

4 plastic zip-lock sandwich bags

Sauté the ground beef in a large pot over medium-high heat until most of the pink is gone. Stir in the onion, cabbage, rice, mint, salt, and pepper and continue to sauté for several minutes longer, or until the onion and cabbage are limp. Remove the pot from the heat and let cool, uncovered, stirring from time to time to hasten cooling.

In a 4-cup jar, pitcher, or lidded container, combine the tomato paste and lemon juice; then blend in the water and tomato sauce. Cover and refrigerate until ready to use.

When the meat mixture is cool, divide it equally among the 4 plastic bags, using about 1⅓ gently-pressed-down cups for each bag. (Don't leave the mixture together in its pot because the rice will continue to expand slightly and measurements will change overnight.) Seal each bag and refrigerate until ready to use—for up to 2 days.

To Cook an Individual Serving

Shake the jar of tomato sauce to blend the mixture; measure out 1 cup plus 1 tablespoon into a small lidded saucepan. Bring the sauce to a boil, uncovered, over medium heat; stir in 1 bag of the beef-rice-cabbage mixture. When the mixture returns to a boil, cover and maintain a steady simmer, lowering the heat just slightly, if necessary, for 15 minutes. Turn off the heat, stir the mixture, quickly return the cover, and let stand for 5 minutes before serving.

To Cook Multiple Servings

Cook following the directions above, using a larger saucepan and multiplying the portions accordingly.

Chicken and Artichoke Hearts in Velvet Avgolemono

Serves 4
Cooking Time: 12 to 15 minutes

8 chicken thighs (about 3
   pounds total weight), or 1¾
   pounds boneless chicken
   thighs
3 or 4 large lemons
Dried dill
2 14-ounce cans artichoke
   hearts

2 large eggs, separated
2 tablespoons cornstarch
1⅔ cups regular-strength
   canned chicken broth
4 tablespoons butter

Remove the skin from each thigh; remove the bones cutting each thigh equally in half as you do to get 16 pieces. Pound piece #1, no plastic covering needed, with a mallet or flat heavy skillet so it is about 25 percent larger than it was originally; don't shred the meat. Put the pounded piece of chicken on a dinner plate; squeeze on some of the juice of 1 lemon (you will use 1 whole lemon on all the chicken pieces); use your fingertips to spread the lemon juice over the surface of the chicken. Top the chicken with a very light sprinkling of dill. Repeat this process for all the chicken pieces, stacking the pounded pieces with lemon and dill in between; make 2 stacks. Cover well and refrigerate until ready to use—for up to 1 day.

Open and drain the cans of artichoke hearts. Cut each heart in half and put them in a bowl; sprinkle on any of the remaining juice from the 1 lemon you used. Cover and refrigerate until ready to use.

In a small mixing bowl, beat the egg whites until you get soft, droopy peaks; stir in the cornstarch until blended; stir in the egg yolks. Squeeze and strain enough juice from the remaining 2 or 3 lemons to measure ½ cup. Stir the lemon juice into the egg mixture until it is smooth; then stir in the chicken broth. Pour this uncooked avgolemono sauce into a 4-cup jar or shake-able container; cover and refrigerate until ready to use.

To Cook an Individual Serving

Heat 1 tablespoon of the butter in a medium-size skillet over medium-high heat. When the bubbling subsides, add 4 pieces of chicken and sauté on both sides until the outsides are whitened. Add 8 artichoke halves, cover, and simmer over medium-low heat for 10 minutes, or until the chicken is just done. Transfer the chicken and artichokes to a dinner plate, leaving the pan juices. Shake the jar of avgolemono sauce; measure out a scant ⅔ cup and pour it into the liquids in the skillet. Raise the heat to medium and stir frequently until the sauce thickens and bubbles. Pour the sauce over the plate of chicken and artichoke hearts and serve.

To Cook Multiple Servings

Multiply portions accordingly using a large skillet if cooking 3 portions at once. Once the chicken and artichokes are cooked, transfer them to a lidded serving dish and set it on the dinner table. Make the avgolemono sauce, pour equal portions into empty dinner plates, and then top with portions of the chicken and artichokes and serve.

Tender Chicken Cutlets in Fresh Mushroom Sauce

Serves 4
Cooking Time: 2 to 4 minutes

6 chicken thighs or 4 chicken
  breast halves
Salt and pepper to taste
1 lemon
8 ounces fresh mushrooms
8 tablespoons (1 stick) butter
2 tablespoons finely chopped
  onion

1 cup regular-strength canned
  chicken broth
2 teaspoons cornstarch
½ cup whole milk or light
  cream
Rice Pilaf (page 213)

Remove the skin and bones from the chicken pieces. If you are using thighs, cut each thigh into 2 equal pieces as you remove the bone to get 12 pieces; if you are using breast halves, slice each breast half in half again to get 8 equal pieces. Sprinkle each prepared chicken piece with salt, pepper, and some lemon juice to taste. Place each chicken piece between generous doubled lengths of plastic wrap. Pound each piece with a heavy mallet or the bottom of a flat heavy skillet until the meat is as thin as you can make it without shredding it. Leave the cutlets in their wrappings and stack them on a dinner plate. Cover the top piece with another piece of plastic wrap and refrigerate until ready to use—for up to 1 day.

Slice the mushrooms thinly to get 3 to 3½ cups; set them aside. Heat 2 tablespoons of the butter in a skillet over medium-high heat. When the bubbling subsides, sauté the onion until soft. Add 2 more tablespoons of butter and the sliced mushrooms; stir and sauté until the mushrooms are limp and cooked. When the mushrooms' juice begins to bubble, remove the skillet from the heat and sprinkle the mushrooms with salt and pepper to taste; then stir in 1 tablespoon of strained fresh lemon juice. Put about half of the mushrooms in a blender container and add the chicken broth; whirl at high speed until completely smooth. Pour the purée back into the skillet of sliced mushrooms and bring to a boil; then lower the heat and simmer, uncovered, stirring from time to time, for 10 to 12 minutes, or until somewhat thickened and reduced by about half.

Blend together the cornstarch and milk; stir it into the simmering sauce and continue stirring until thickened. Remove the skillet from the heat and let cool, uncovered, to room temperature, stirring from time to time. Store, refrigerated, in a covered container.

Make the Rice Pilaf to be used as a side dish. Once cool, cover and refrigerate until ready to use.

To Cook an Individual Serving

Prepare 1 portion of the Rice Pilaf following the directions on page 214; cover and set aside.

In a skillet, melt 1 tablespoon of butter over medium-high heat. When the bubbling subsides, add 3 unwrapped thigh cutlets (or 2 unwrapped breast cutlets) and sauté for a minute or two on each side until no more rosiness remains; don't overcook them. Put the cutlets on a dinner plate along with a portion of Rice Pilaf.

Measure between ⅓ and ½ cup of the mushroom sauce into the hot skillet; heat and stir for several minutes, until it is smooth and simmering. Pour the sauce over the cooked chicken and serve immediately.

To Cook Multiple Servings

Prepare the pilaf, cutlets, and sauce as directed, multiplying portions accordingly.

Variations:

MUSHROOM SAUCE WITH WINE

Replace the milk with ½ cup of dry white wine.

MUSHROOM-MARSALA SAUCE

Increase the chicken broth to 1¼ cups. Replace the milk with ¼ cup of Marsala wine.

MUSHROOM SAUCE PICCANTE

Replace the milk with an additional ¼ cup of chicken broth. Thicken the sauce as directed and let it cool completely: It will seem overly thick. Once cooled, stir in ¼ cup of strained fresh lemon juice and 1 teaspoon of grated lemon rind.

Green Bean and Bacon Soup

Serves 4
Cooking Time: 1 minute

This soup is a favorite with my family and an especially tasty way to use fresh green beans. Even a child can assemble and cook a portion in less than 2 minutes.

1 pound sliced bacon
2½ to 3 cups cut fresh green beans, or 1 10-ounce package frozen green beans, thawed and drained
3 cups peeled potatoes cut into ¾-inch dice
Salt and pepper to taste
½ cup chopped scallions
2½ tablespoons cornstarch

3 13¾-ounce cans regular-strength chicken broth
2 teaspoons tomato paste
⅓ cup minced fresh parsley leaves
1 loaf crusty Italian bread

4 zip-lock plastic sandwich bags, or 4 12-ounce plastic containers

Cut the package of bacon across the slices into 3 sections. Separate the slices in the first section and fry them in a medium-size skillet over medium-high heat until just crisp. Drain the bacon on several paper towels placed on top of a layer of newspaper. Fry the rest of the bacon sections together; drain as you did the first section.

Add the green beans to the hot bacon drippings; stir and sauté for about 6 to 8 minutes, or until they pass the bright-green stage and are about a minute away from being completely cooked. If you are using frozen green beans, sauté only for 1 to 2 minutes. Remove all the green beans with a slotted spoon; drain on layers of paper towels on top of newspaper.

Lower the heat to medium; add the potatoes and sauté, stirring frequently, for 7 to 8 minutes, or until the potatoes are just done. Remove with a slotted spoon; drain on layers of paper towels on top of newspaper; sprinkle with salt and pepper to taste.

Measure 3 tablespoons of the bacon drippings from the skillet into a clean medium-to-large saucepan; add the scallions and sauté for a few minutes until they are limp. Remove all the scallions with a slotted spoon; place them in a small bowl and set aside.

Remove the saucepan from the heat and whisk in the cornstarch until it has been absorbed. Return the pan to the heat; stir briefly and then add the chicken broth, stirring well to blend in the cornstarch. Mix in the tomato paste and bring to a boil so that the cornstarch thickens and clears; remove the pan from the heat; cover and let cool.

Divide the bacon, green beans, and potatoes each into 4 equal piles. Put 1 pile of the potatoes in the bottom of a 12- or 16-ounce plastic container or a zip-lock sandwich bag; add 1 teaspoon of the sautéed scallions and top with 1 pile of green beans; sprinkle 1 tablespoon of parsley over the green beans; place 1 pile of bacon on top; seal the container. Repeat, making 4 containers or bags. Refrigerate until ready to use—for up to 2 days. Pour the cooled broth into a 5-cup pitcher or container, cover, and refrigerate.

To Cook an Individual Serving

Measure 1¼ cups of the broth into a saucepan and bring to a boil over medium-high heat. Add 1 portion of the bacon-green beans-potatoes mixture and return to a boil; lower the heat and simmer for a minute, or until heated through. Serve with a hunk of crusty bread.

To Cook Multiple Servings

Cook following the directions above, combining 1¼ cups broth and 1 portion for each serving. Warm the bread in a 250-degree oven for 10 minutes before serving it along with the soup.

Pork Cutlets in Spiced Salsa

Serves 4
Cooking Time: 4 to 5 minutes

8 small-to-medium pork chops,
   about ½ to ¾ inch thick
1 cup all-purpose flour
2 large eggs
1 teaspoon salt
¼ teaspoon pepper
2 cups fine dry bread crumbs
1 ½ tablespoons corn oil
1 small onion, finely chopped
1 garlic clove, smashed and
   finely minced
2 ½ cups ripe tomatoes,
   peeled, seeded, and finely
   chopped

½ teaspoon sugar
1 ½ to 3 tablespoons finely
   chopped, stemmed, and
   seeded jalapeño or serrano
   chiles
1 ½ tablespoons strained fresh
   lime juice
1 tablespoon minced fresh
   parsley leaves
4 tablespoons butter
4 tablespoons olive oil

Remove the bones from the chops and trim away the excess fat from the outer rim. Place each chop between generous doubled lengths of plastic wrap. Pound each piece with a heavy mallet or the bottom of a flat heavy skillet until the meat is thin but not torn. Set the still-wrapped cutlets aside.

Put ⅓ cup of the flour into a shallow soup bowl for dredging. In a second shallow bowl, beat the eggs until bubbly. In a third, larger bowl, blend together the remaining ⅔ cup of flour with the salt, pepper, and 1¼ cups of the bread crumbs; sprinkle a large, rimmed baking sheet with the remaining ¾ cup of bread crumbs; set the baking sheet aside.

Unwrap the first pounded pork chop and dip it, on both sides, in the plain dredging flour, shaking off any excess flour. Dip the meat in the beaten eggs so that both sides are well coated; then thoroughly coat the piece on both sides with the bread crumb mixture. Put the coated piece on the baking sheet. Coat all the chops in this manner; cover the baking sheet with plastic wrap and refrigerate until ready to use—for up to 1 day.

Heat the corn oil in a small saucepan over medium-high heat; add the onion and garlic and sauté until they are limp. Stir in the tomatoes, sugar, chiles, and salt to taste; simmer gently, uncovered, for 15 minutes, or until thickened to your liking. Remove from the heat; stir in the lime juice and parsley; let cool, uncovered, to room temperature. Cover and refrigerate until ready to use.

To Cook an Individual Serving

Heat 1 tablespoon of butter and 1 tablespoon of olive oil in a medium-size skillet over medium-high heat. When the butter and oil just begin to bubble, add 2 of the breaded pork cutlets and sauté for 4 to 5 minutes on each side, or until they are nicely browned and just tender. Place the cutlets on a dinner plate.

Spoon about ⅓ cup of the salsa into the hot skillet and stir until heated through; spoon over the center of each cutlet and serve immediately.

To Cook Multiple Servings

Heat 1 tablespoon of butter and 1 tablespoon of oil for every 2 cutlets, using a larger skillet. Cook the cutlets and salsa as directed above.

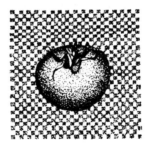

Two-Minute Fish Fillets in Shrimp Sauce

Serves 4
Cooking Time: 2 minutes

1 to 1½ pounds thin boneless
  fish fillets, such as sole,
  flounder, or perch
½ pound medium-size shrimp,
  peeled and deveined if fresh
2 tablespoons butter
1 tablespoon grated onion
1 tablespoon all-purpose flour

½ cup bottled clam juice
1 tablespoon tomato paste
1 cup heavy cream
⅛ to ¼ teaspoon cayenne
  pepper
Salt and pepper to taste
Rice Pilaf (page 213)
Butter for greasing the pan

Thaw the fish, if frozen, and separate it into 4 equal portions. Measure the thickest fillet at its thickest point: It will probably be about ¼-inch thick, but if it measures closer to ½ inch, you must remember to increase the cooking time by 2 to 3 minutes more. Wrap each serving portion in plastic wrap and refrigerate until ready to use—for up to 1 day.

If using frozen shrimp, drop them into a bowl of hot tap water until they are just thawed. Rinse the shrimp, fresh or thawed, several times in cold running water; then drain. Cut each shrimp in half, lengthwise, and set them aside.

Heat the butter in a saucepan over medium-high heat. When the bubbling subsides, add the grated onion and sauté until it is soft but not browned. Remove the pan from the heat and stir in the flour until it has been absorbed. Return the pan to low-to-medium heat and slowly whisk in the clam juice until smooth; blend in the tomato paste and then the cream. Slowly bring the sauce to a boil until it is thickened; then stir in the shrimp, cayenne pepper, and salt and pepper to taste. Lower the heat and simmer, uncovered, for about 3 minutes, or until thickened to your liking. Remove the saucepan from the heat and let the sauce cool, uncovered, to room temperature, stirring from time to time. Store, refrigerated, in a covered container.

Make the Rice Pilaf to be used as a side dish, if you like. Once cool, cover and refrigerate until ready to use.

To Cook an Individual Serving

Prepare 1 portion of the Rice Pilaf following the directions on page 214; cover and set it aside.

Preheat the oven to 500 degrees. Lightly butter the bottom of a small baking pan. Unwrap 1 portion of the refrigerated fish; arrange the fish pieces, skin side down, on the buttered pan; moisten the tops of each fish piece by patting with water from your fingers. Set the pan aside.

Stir up the sauce to distribute the shrimp; spoon ½ cup into a small saucepan and bring to a simmer over medium heat; stir and turn the heat to low.

Put the pan of fish on the lowest oven rack and bake for 2 to 2½ minutes, or until the fish has just turned flaky at the center. If your fish measured thicker than ¼ inch, add 2 to 2½ minutes more baking time for every ¼ inch.

Pour the sauce onto a dinner plate; arrange the fish on top of the sauce and the pilaf to the side. Serve immediately.

To Cook Multiple Servings

Prepare the Rice Pilaf in the portions you need. Arrange the fish portions, snugly, side by side on a larger buttered baking sheet, but do not overlap the fillets except for some end edges. Use ½ cup of sauce for each portion. Bake the fish as directed above.

Ready-to-Pour Quiches with Ham and Cheese

Serves 4
Cooking Time: 25 minutes

PASTRY CRUST
2⅔ cups all-purpose flour
1 teaspoon salt
16 tablespoons (2 sticks) cold
  butter
1 large egg
1 average-size ice cube

QUICHE FILLING
6 ounces boiled ham
1 medium-size onion
1½ tablespoons butter
Pepper to taste
4 ounces Monterey Jack or
  Gouda cheese
2 tablespoons grated Parmesan
  cheese
5 large eggs
About 1½ cups heavy or light
  cream

4 aluminum foil "roll pans"
  (8 by 5 by 1 inch)

MAKE THE PASTRY CRUSTS: Lightly spoon the flour into a mixing bowl; mix in the salt. Cut the 2 sticks of butter into bits; separate
them and mix them into the flour until they are coated. Use a pastry
blender to incorporate the butter into the flour until the mixture
looks somewhat like lumpy cornmeal. Cover and refrigerate the bowl
for at least 45 minutes. In the meantime, lightly beat the egg; pour
it into a 1-cup measuring cup; add the ice cube and then add enough
cold water to measure ⅔ cup, not counting the froth on top. Cover
and refrigerate.

MAKE THE QUICHE FILLING: Slice the ham into 1½-inch-long
julienne matchsticks (you will need 1¼ cups). Slice the onion in
half; then slice each half thinly to get ¾ to 1 cup separated half-
circles. Heat 1½ tablespoons of the butter in a skillet over medium-
high heat; add the onion and sauté until limp. Then add the ham
and continue to sauté until the ham is limp and rosy and the onion
is stringy but not browned. Spread the ham and onion mixture on a
dinner plate to cool; sprinkle with pepper to taste.
  Shred the Monterey Jack cheese to get 1 closely packed cup; mix
in the Parmesan cheese and set the mixture aside. Break the 5 eggs

into a 4-cup measuring cup; beat lightly but not until frothy. Add enough cream to make 2½ cups. Mix with a fork; then mix in the cheese and then the ham. Cover and refrigerate until ready to use—for up to 1 day.

Preheat the oven to 450 degrees. Take the bowl of flour-butter and the cup of egg-water out of the refrigerator. Remove the ice cube from the egg-water; stir to blend and then pour about half into the bowl of flour-butter. Use 2 forks to toss and combine, adding more egg-water 1 tablespoon at a time, until the mixture looks like it wants to stick together without being sticky. Working quickly, form the mixture into a ball of coarse dough; cut it into 4 equal pieces; refrigerate all but one piece.

Roll out the first dough portion on a lightly floured surface into a rectangle about 10 by 13 inches. Place the dough in 1 roll pan so that the dough overlaps the rim by a full inch. Rather than fluting the dough around the rim, tuck it around the outside of the pan, right to the bottom; pinch to secure the outside corners (this will prevent the dough from shrinking to the bottom during baking time). Prick the inside bottom and sides with a fork. Repeat this process for the next dough portion. Place 2 pastry-lined pans on a baking sheet. Bake for 12 to 15 minutes, or until light golden; remove carefully and allow to cool. Repeat for the remaining 2 dough portions. Once cool, gently break the outside crusts off at the rim of each pan. Stack the pastry pans, wrap in a plastic bag, and refrigerate until ready to use.

To Cook an Individual Serving

Preheat the oven to 375 degrees. Unwrap 1 pastry crust. Stir up the quiche filling from the bottom; ladle 1 measured cup into the crust. Bake for 25 minutes, or until set and browned. Slide the quiche out of its pan and onto a dinner plate and serve.

To Cook Multiple Servings

Cook following the directions above.

STIR-FRIED SUPPERS

The raw, prepared ingredients for these meals wait in the refrigerator to be cooked in minutes. The recipes are both American and Chinese.

Tender Chicken with Mushrooms and Pea Pods

Melt-in-Your-Mouth Chicken Strips in Fresh Herbs

Chicken al Diavolo

Spiced Szechuan Chicken with Ramen Noodles

Chicken Marsala with Mushrooms and Ham

Chicken and Potatoes with Lemon and Oregano

Crispy Barbecued Pork and Corn

Pork Lo Mein

Michigan Steak and Potatoes

Hot-and-Sour Flank Steak with Fried Rice

Beef with Red Wine and Mushrooms

Lemon-Ginger Shrimp with Pea Pods

Tender Chicken with Mushrooms and Pea Pods

Serves 4
Cooking Time: 10 minutes

The method here calls for marinating the chicken pieces in a tenderizing mixture and then parboiling them. This yields extremely tender chicken that stores well until you are ready to stir-fry it.

2 whole chicken breasts (about 2½ pounds total weight), or 1 to 1½ pounds boneless chicken
1 large egg white
1 tablespoon corn oil
7 teaspoons cornstarch
¼ teaspoon baking soda
1 6-ounce package frozen pea pods
12 ounces fresh mushrooms
1 cup regular-strength canned chicken broth

1 tablespoon plus 2 teaspoons soy sauce
1½ tablespoons fresh lemon juice
1 teaspoon ground ginger
Rice Pilaf (page 213), or 1 5-ounce can chow mein noodles, or both the rice and the noodles
4 tablespoons oil for cooking

Remove and discard the skin and bones from the chicken. Cut the meat into pieces that are about 2 or 3 inches long, ¾ inch wide, and ¼ inch thick; set the chicken aside. In a medium-size mixing bowl, lightly beat the egg white until foamy; blend in the corn oil, 2 teaspoons of the cornstarch, and the baking soda. Add the chicken pieces to this mixture and stir until all the pieces are coated on all sides; set aside at room temperature for 10 to 30 minutes.

In the meantime, thaw the pea pods at room temperature; once thawed, refrigerate them. Slice the mushrooms into ¼-inch-thick slices; wrap well and refrigerate. Combine the chicken broth, the remaining 5 teaspoons of cornstarch, and 1 tablespoon of the soy sauce in a jar; cover, shake briefly, and refrigerate.

Bring 2 quarts of water to a steady boil over high heat; add the chicken and cook, stirring and lowering the heat as necessary, for 1 minute, or until the chicken is no longer pink; be careful not to overcook it; drain in a colander for 1 minute; then put the pieces into a bowl. In a small bowl, combine the lemon juice, 2 teaspoons of soy sauce, and the ginger; mix this into the warm chicken and let cool, uncovered. Once cool, cover the chicken with plastic wrap or aluminum foil and refrigerate, along with the other ingredients, until ready to use—for up to 2 days.

If you want rice with this dish, prepare it and then refrigerate it until needed.

To Cook an Individual Serving

Heat up the rice following the directions on page 214; have the can of chow mein noodles handy, if you prefer.

Heat 1 tablespoon of oil in a skillet or a wok over high heat. Add 1⅓ cups of the mushrooms; stir and toss as you sauté them for 2 minutes, or until they look half cooked. Lower the heat to medium-high and add ½ cup of the chicken, sauté, stirring constantly, for 1 minute only. Shake the sauce in the jar and pour in ¼ cup; when it boils, sprinkle one fourth of the thawed pea pods on top. Leave the mixture, untouched, until it bubbles and thickens; then gently stir the pea pods into the mixture, simmer for only 15 seconds, and serve immediately over the rice and/or noodles.

To Cook Multiple Servings

Cook following the directions above, using 1⅓ cups of mushrooms, ½ cup of chicken, ¼ cup of sauce, and one fourth of the pea pods for each serving.

Melt-in-Your-Mouth Chicken Strips in Fresh Herbs

Serves 4
Cooking Time: 12 minutes

8 chicken thighs (about 3 pounds total weight), or 1 ½ pounds boneless chicken	1 large egg white
3 tablespoons cornstarch	4 tablespoons butter
½ teaspoon salt	½ cup finely snipped fresh parsley leaves
½ teaspoon pepper	2 tablespoons minced fresh or freeze-dried chives
2 tablespoons oil	1 lemon

Remove and discard the skin and bones from the chicken. Slice the meat into long strips that are ½ inch wide; put the strips in a medium-size mixing bowl and set them aside. In a small bowl or cup, combine the cornstarch, salt, and pepper; mix in the oil and then drizzle the mixture into the bowl of chicken. Use your fingers to work the mixture into the chicken so that each strip is coated. Cover with plastic wrap or aluminum foil and set aside at room temperature for 30 minutes to 2 hours.

Beat the egg white until foamy; mix it into the chicken strips; then refrigerate until ready to use—for up to 1 day.

To Cook an Individual Serving

Heat 1 tablespoon of butter in a skillet over medium-high heat. When it bubbles, add a scant cup of chicken strips. Use 2 metal spatulas to stir the chicken into 1 layer; then sauté for about 10 minutes, turning the pieces from time to time, until the chicken is white throughout and a golden crispy-brown on all sides. Stir in 2 tablespoons of the parsley and ½ tablespoon of the chives, followed by a squeeze or two of lemon juice. Transfer to a dinner plate with a slotted spoon; serve immediately with a side dish from Chapter 11 (pages 211–21).

To Cook Multiple Servings

Cook following the directions above, multiplying the portions accordingly. If you are cooking 3 or 4 portions together, use only 3 tablespoons of butter.

Chicken al Diavolo

Serves 4
Cooking Time: 10 to 20 minutes

2 whole chicken breasts (about
   3 pounds total weight), or
   1 ½ pounds boneless chicken
1 medium-size onion
2 garlic cloves
¼ plus ⅛ teaspoon cayenne
   pepper

2 tablespoons snipped fresh
   parsley leaves
4 tablespoons olive oil
½ cup canned tomato sauce
1 lemon

ACCOMPANIMENT
**Crusty Italian bread or cooked
spaghetti**

Remove and discard the skin and bones from the chicken; then cut the meat into long strips about 1½ inch wide. On a slant, cut the strips into small slices at ½-inch intervals. Place in a container, cover, and refrigerate until ready to use—for up to 1½ days.

Chop the onion to get ½ cup; smash and very finely mince the garlic; mix the garlic thoroughly into the onion; then mix in the cayenne pepper and parsley. Cover and refrigerate until needed.

To Cook an Individual Serving

Prepare 1 portion of spaghetti following the package directions or else cut off a few generous slices of crusty Italian bread. Heat 1 tablespoon of olive oil in a small skillet over medium-high heat; add 3 tablespoons of the onion mixture and sauté for 2 minutes, or until the onion is limp. Add ½ cup of the chicken and sauté for about 3 minutes, stirring frequently, or until the chicken has just cooked through. Stir in 2 tablespoons of tomato sauce and simmer for 1 to 2 minutes, or until thickened. Remove the skillet from the heat and sprinkle with a squeeze of lemon juice. Serve either with hunks of crusty Italian bread for sauce-dipping or over a bed of generously buttered and salted spaghetti.

To Cook Multiple Servings

Use a 10-inch skillet and cook, following the directions above, multiplying the portions accordingly. If you are cooking 4 portions at once, use only 3 tablespoons of olive oil.

Spiced Szechuan Chicken with Oriental Noodles

Serves 4
Cooking Time: 10 minutes

2 whole chicken breasts (about
2 ½ pounds total weight), or
1 ½ pounds boneless chicken
3 ½ tablespoons corn oil
2 3-ounce packages Oriental
noodle soup mix, chicken or
mushroom flavor

5 teaspoons cornstarch
1 teaspoon celery seed
½ teaspoon ground ginger
¼ teaspoon cayenne pepper
1 cup strained fresh orange
juice
4 tablespoons soy sauce

Remove and discard the skin and bones from the chicken; then cut the meat into long strips about 1 ½ inches wide. On a slant, cut the strips into small slices at ½-inch intervals. Place in a container and mix in 2 tablespoons of the oil so that all the pieces are coated. Cover and refrigerate until ready to use—for up to 1 ½ days.

When ready to cook, bring 3 quarts of water to a steady boil. Open the packages of noodles and set the 2 seasoning packets aside. Break each block of noodles into quarters and drop them into the boiling water; boil for only 2 minutes (even though the package will tell you 3 minutes) stirring the noodles frequently to separate them. Pour the noodles into a colander and rinse with hot tap water; toss and let drain for 2 minutes. In the meantime, mix together the remaining 1 ½ tablespoons of corn oil with the contents of the 2 seasoning packets. Pour the still-warm, drained noodles into a medium-size bowl; drizzle the seasoned oil on top and use your fingers to coat all the noodles with the oil. Cover and refrigerate until needed.

Combine the remaining ingredients in the order listed in a jar. Cover, shake to blend, and refrigerate until needed.

To Cook an Individual Serving

Place a small skillet over medium-high heat; add ½ cup of the cooked noodles and stir-fry for several minutes, or until the noodles are heated through. Slide the noodles onto a dinner plate and set it aside.

Return the skillet to the heat and add ½ cup of the chicken pieces; stir-fry for 2 to 3 minutes, or just until no pink remains. Quickly shake the sauce in its jar, measure out ¼ cup, and pour it over the chicken. Once the sauce has thickened, let it simmer for 1 minute and then pour the contents of the skillet over the plate of noodles and serve immediately.

To Cook Multiple Servings

Cook following the directions above, using a larger skillet or a wok and multiplying the portions accordingly. Either serve out individual portions of the noodles and chicken on dinner plates or serve the noodles in one serving dish and the sauced chicken in another.

Chicken Marsala with Mushrooms and Ham

Serves 4
Cooking Time: 10 minutes

6 to 8 chicken thighs (about
  2½ pounds total weight), or
  1 to 1½ pounds boneless
  chicken
6 ounces sliced boiled ham
4 tablespoons olive oil
¼ teaspoon salt
Pepper to taste

12 ounces fresh mushrooms
2 tablespoons plus 1 teaspoon
  all-purpose flour
½ cup Marsala wine
½ cup regular-strength canned
  chicken broth
4 tablespoons butter

Remove and discard the skin and bones from the chicken; cut the meat into strips about 1½ to 2 inches wide; then cut the strips on a slant into small slices at ½-inch intervals. Put the chicken pieces in a medium-size bowl or container. Cut the ham slices into 2-inch-long julienne matchsticks (you will need about 1 cup); separate the pieces and gently mix them into the chicken. Add to this mixture the olive oil, salt, and pepper and mix gently; then cover and refrigerate until ready to use—for up to 1½ days.

Cut the mushrooms into ¼-inch-thick slices (you will need about 5⅓ cups); wrap well and refrigerate. Combine the flour, Marsala, and chicken broth in a jar and shake until smooth; then cover and refrigerate until needed.

To Cook an Individual Serving

Melt 1 tablespoon of the butter in a small skillet over medium-high heat. When the bubbling subsides, add 1⅓ cups of the sliced mushrooms and stir-fry for about 2 minutes, or until they look only half-cooked and not quite limp.

Add 1 scant cup of the chicken-ham mixture and stir-fry, turning the pieces frequently, for about 5 minutes, or until the chicken is cooked just past the pink stage.

Shake the Marsala mixture in the jar, measure out ¼ cup, and pour it into the skillet. Continue cooking for 1 to 2 more minutes, or until thickened and all the alcohol has burned off. Serve immediately.

To Cook Multiple Servings

Cook following the directions above, using a larger skillet and multiplying the portions accordingly.

Chicken and Potatoes with Lemon and Oregano

Serves 4
Cooking Time: 15 minutes

6 to 8 chicken thighs (about
  2½ pounds total weight), or
  1 to 1½ pounds boneless
  chicken
About 3 lemons
1 large garlic clove, smashed
  and very finely minced
1½ teaspoons dried oregano

1 teaspoon salt
¼ teaspoon pepper
1 small-to-medium-size onion
6 medium-size, or 4 large,
  potatoes, peeled
4 tablespoons butter, melted
4 tablespoons butter

Remove and discard the skin and bones from the chicken; cut the meat into strips about 1½ to 2 inches wide; then cut the strips on a slant into small slices at ½-inch intervals. Put equal portions of the chicken pieces into 4 6-ounce cups or glasses; set them aside. Squeeze the lemons to get ½ cup of fresh lemon juice; mix in the garlic, oregano, ½ teaspoon of the salt, and the pepper. Drizzle 2 tablespoons of this marinade over each of the 4 cups or glasses of chicken. Cover each cup or glass with plastic wrap or aluminum foil and refrigerate until ready to use—for up to 1½ days. Peel and chop the onion to get ½ cup; cover and refrigerate until needed.

Boil the whole potatoes, uncovered, for about 20 minutes, or until the largest potato, when pierced at the center, tests done. Pour out the boiling water and replace it with cold water to cover; let sit for 10 minutes; then drain and cut the potatoes into 1-inch cubes. Measure the cup amount of cubed potatoes (it will be from 5 to 7 cups); divide the cup number by four; make a small note of the divided number and tape it to a bowl or container. Put the potatoes into that bowl; toss in the remaining ½ teaspoon of salt and the melted butter. Cover with plastic wrap or aluminum foil and refrigerate until needed.

To Cook an Individual Serving

Heat 1 tablespoon of the butter in a small skillet over medium-high heat. When the bubbling subsides, add 2 tablespoons of the onion and sauté for 1 to 2 minutes, or until the onion is limp and the butter returns to a sizzle. Refer to the potato measurement taped to the potato container and add that amount to the skillet; stir to coat all the potato cubes with butter. Sauté the potatoes for about 5 minutes, gently turning them from time to time.

When the potatoes are heated through, add only the chicken pieces from 1 of the 4 containers, reserving the marinade. Stir-fry the chicken for about 5 minutes, gently turning the pieces 2 or 3 times during this time, until the chicken is just cooked through and no longer pink. Pour the reserved marinade into the skillet; let the contents return to a boil for a minute, so that the sauce can thicken; then serve.

To Cook Multiple Servings

Cook following the directions above, using a larger skillet and multiplying the portions accordingly.

Crispy Barbecued Pork and Corn

Serves 4
Cooking Time: 15 minutes

1½ pounds boneless pork, or 8
  pork chops, each about ¾
  inch thick
5 tablespoons cornstarch
¼ teaspoon cayenne pepper
2 tablespoons oil

1 large egg white
2 10-ounce packages frozen
  corn
⅔ cup bottled barbecue sauce
6 tablespoons butter

Trim the fat from the pork (and remove the bones if you are using chops). On a slant and across the grain, cut the pork into the thinnest possible slices, about 1 to 2 inches long; set the meat aside on your cutting board. In a medium-size mixing bowl, combine the cornstarch and cayenne pepper; mix in the oil to get a smooth paste. Beat the egg white until foamy and blend it into the cornstarch paste. Add the pork to this mixture working the mixture into the meat with your fingers, so that each slice is coated. Cover the surface of the meat directly with plastic wrap and refrigerate until ready to use—for up to 1 day.

Pour the frozen corn into a medium-size mixing bowl and stir in the barbecue sauce; cover with plastic wrap or aluminum foil and refrigerate.

To Cook an Individual Serving

Melt 1½ tablespoons of the butter in a skillet over medium-high heat. When it bubbles, add 1 cup of the pork. Stir the meat into 1 layer, turning the pieces from time to time, for about 10 to 12 minutes, or until the pork is cooked and crispy-brown. Stir the corn-barbecue sauce mixture; measure out 1 heaping cup and pour it into the skillet. Heat for 1 minute and then serve.

To Cook Multiple Servings

Cook following the directions above, multiplying the portions accordingly.

Pork Lo Mein

Serves 4
Cooking Time: about 10 minutes

3 3-ounce packages Oriental
   noodle soup mix, pork or
   Oriental flavor
2 tablespoons corn oil
1 ½ pounds boneless pork, or 8
   pork chops, each about ¾
   inch thick
4 scallions

12 ounces fresh mushrooms
1 6-ounce package frozen pea
   pods
1 8-ounce can whole water
   chestnuts
8 tablespoons corn oil for
   cooking
3 tablespoons soy sauce

Bring 3 or 4 quarts of water to a steady boil. Open the packages
of noodles and set the 3 flavor packets aside. Break each block of
noodles into quarters and drop them into the boiling water; boil for
only 2 minutes (even though the package will tell you 3 minutes);
stir the noodles all the while to separate them. Pour the noodles into
a colander and rinse them with hot tap water; toss and let drain for
2 minutes. In the meantime, mix together the 2 tablespoons of corn
oil with the contents of the 3 flavor packets. Pour the still-warm,
drained noodles into a medium-size bowl and drizzle the flavored oil
on top; use your fingers to coat all the noodles with the oil. Cover
with plastic wrap or aluminum foil and refrigerate until ready to use.

Trim the fat from the pork (and remove the bones if you are using
chops). On a slant and across the grain, cut the pork into the thinnest possible slices, about 1 to 2 inches long. Chop the scallions
about 2 inches into the green part to get about ⅓ cup; toss the
scallions with the pork in a bowl; cover with plastic wrap or aluminum foil and refrigerate until ready to use—for up to 1 ½ days.

Cut the mushrooms into ¼-inch-thick slices; cover well and refrigerate. Let the package of pea pods thaw and then refrigerate it.
Drain the liquid from the can of water chestnuts into a small storage
container; cut the water chestnuts into slices and return the slices to
the can liquid in the storage container; refrigerate until needed.

To Cook an Individual Serving

Heat 2 tablespoons of oil in a skillet or a wok over high heat. When a drop of water flicked into the oil sizzles, add 1 cup of the pork-scallion mixture. Use 2 metal spatulas to stir and toss the meat until it is only half-cooked: The pork will be tinged with white but raw in the center. Lower the heat to medium-high, add 3 tablespoons of the sliced water chestnuts and 1⅓ cups of the mushrooms; continue to stir and cook until the pork turns white. Stir in 1 scant cup of the noodles, mixing them in evenly. Sprinkle one fourth of the pea pods on top of the mixture and sprinkle with 2 teaspoons of soy sauce; toss and cook for only a minute or two, or until the pea pods are just tender and the noodles are heated through. Serve immediately.

To Cook Multiple Servings

Cook following the directions above, multiplying the portions accordingly.

Michigan Steak and Potatoes

Serves 4
Cooking Time: 20 minutes

6 medium-size, or 4 large,
   potatoes, peeled
1 ½ teaspoons salt
¾ teaspoon pepper
3 tablespoons butter, melted

1 ½ to 2 pounds boneless
   chuck steak
1 ⅓ cups chopped onion
8 tablespoons bacon drippings

Boil the whole potatoes, uncovered, for about 20 minutes, or until the largest potato, when pierced at the center, tests done. Pour out the boiling water and replace it with cold water to cover; let sit for 10 minutes; then drain and cut the potatoes into ½-inch dice. Measure the cup amount of diced potatoes (it will be from 5 to 7 cups); divide the cup number by four; make a small note of the divided number and tape it to a bowl or storage container; put the potatoes into that bowl; toss in ½ teaspoon of the salt and ¼ teaspoon of the pepper and the melted butter. Cover with plastic wrap or aluminum foil and refrigerate until needed.

Trim the excess fat from the steak; then cut the meat into ¼- to ½-inch dice. Put the meat into a bowl and mix in the remaining 1 teaspoon of salt and ½ teaspoon of pepper; cover with plastic wrap or aluminum foil and refrigerate until ready to use—for up to 2 days.

Put the chopped onion in a small storage bag or container and refrigerate until needed.

To Cook an Individual Serving

Melt 2 tablespoons of the bacon drippings in a small heavy (cast-iron, if you have) skillet over medium-high heat. When a drop of water flicked into the hot fat sizzles, add ⅓ cup of the onion and sauté for 1 to 2 minutes, or until the onion is limp and the fat returns to a sizzle. Refer to the potato measurement taped to the potato container and add that amount to the skillet; stir to coat all the potatoes with the bacon drippings. When the bubbling sizzle returns, sauté the potatoes for about 10 minutes, gently turning them once or twice during this time. When the potatoes begin to brown, stir in 1 cup of the diced steak and cook for 2 to 5 minutes more, or until the steak is either pinkish (for medium-rare, as it will continue to cook on its own) or just past losing all its pink (for medium to well-done), according to your liking. Serve at once.

To Cook Multiple Servings

Use a 10-inch skillet for 2 or more servings. Cook following the directions above, multiplying the portions accordingly. If you are cooking 4 portions at once, use only 6 tablespoons of bacon drippings.

Hot-and-Sour Flank Steak with Fried Rice

Serves 4
Cooking Time: 8 to 10 minutes

1 ½ pounds flank steak
7 tablespoons corn oil
1 ½ cups plus 2 tablespoons
  water
4 tablespoons soy sauce
1 cup long-grain converted
  rice

7 to 8 scallions
3 tablespoons light brown
  sugar
½ teaspoon ground ginger
¼ teaspoon cayenne pepper
2 teaspoons vinegar
2 large garlic cloves

Following the lines of the grain of the meat, cut the flank steak 3 inches wide; then cut these lengths across the grain and at a slant into ½-inch-thick slices. In a bowl, mix 2 tablespoons of the oil into the steak slices, so that each piece is coated; cover with plastic wrap or aluminum foil and refrigerate until ready to use—for up to 1 ½ days.

Bring 1 ½ cups of water, 3 tablespoons of the oil, and 2 table-spoons of the soy sauce to a boil in a saucepan; stir in the rice, cover, and simmer for 20 minutes; let the rice sit in its pan, without uncovering, for 10 minutes. Uncover the rice, spread it over 2 dinner plates, to let it cool, uncovered.

In the meantime, chop the scallions 2 inches into the green part to get ½ cup; mix the chopped scallions into the rice. Once the rice has cooled, put it into a bowl or container; cover and refrigerate until needed.

To make the hot-and-sour sauce, combine the brown sugar, ginger, cayenne pepper, the remaining 2 tablespoons of soy sauce, 2 tablespoons of water, and the vinegar in a cup or small bowl; mix well and set aside. Put the remaining 2 tablespoons of oil in a small saucepan or skillet over medium heat. Peel and smash but do not chop the garlic; add it to the hot oil and let it sizzle, turning it once, until it is crispy-brown on both sides; remove and discard the garlic. Re-blend the sauce mixture and, being very careful to stand way back from the stove, quickly pour about half of the sauce mixture into the garlic-flavored oil; then quickly step away while the spurting and bubbling subside. Pour the rest of the sauce mixture into the pan and cook and stir down the bubbles for 1 minute; then remove the pan from the heat and allow the sauce to cool. Once cool, pour the sauce into a cup, cover, and refrigerate until needed.

To Cook an Individual Serving

Measure 1 cup of the rice into a small skillet; put the skillet over medium-high heat and stir-fry the rice, turning occasionally, for about 5 minutes, or until the scallions are limp; transfer the fried rice to an individual dinner plate.

With the skillet off the heat, lay the steak strips over the skillet's surface, much as you would prepare the bacon; return the skillet to high heat and cook the meat for about 2 minutes, turning the strips once, until the meat is no more than juicy-rare. (Even if you don't like your meat rare, it will continue to cook on its own to medium doneness.) Quickly lay the steak strips on top of the fried rice on the dinner plate. Return the skillet with the steak drippings to the heat; stir in 1 tablespoon of the hot-and-sour sauce and let it bubble and thicken for 30 seconds. Pour this sauce over the steak strips and serve immediately.

To Cook Multiple Servings

Cook following the directions above, using a larger skillet or a wok, and multiplying the portions accordingly. Apportion the rice, then the steak, and then the sauce onto separate dinner plates and serve immediately so that the steak does not become overdone.

Beef with Red Wine and Mushrooms

Serves 4
Cooking Time: 5 to 10 minutes

1 ½ pounds boneless chuck
   steak
½ teaspoon pepper
½ teaspoon salt, optional
2 tablespoons olive oil
1 medium-size onion

12 ounces fresh mushrooms
3 tablespoons cornstarch
1 10½-ounce can undiluted
   condensed beef consommé
⅔ cup dry red wine
4 tablespoons butter

ACCOMPANIMENT
4 portions egg noodles

Trim any excess fat from the steak. Cut the meat into long strips
1 ½ to 2 inches wide; then cut the strips, at a slant and across the
grain, into ¼-inch slices. In a bowl, use your fingers to mix in the
pepper, salt, and olive oil; store in either a covered bowl or in a
plastic food storage bag. Refrigerate until ready to use—for up to 2
days.

Peel and halve the onion; cut each half into the thinnest possible
slices; separate the half-rings. When you have about 1⅓ cups of
half-rings, cover with plastic wrap or aluminum foil and refrigerate
until needed. Cut the mushrooms into ¼-inch-thick slices; cover
and refrigerate until needed. Combine the cornstarch, consommé,
and wine in a jar; cover, shake to blend, and refrigerate until needed.

To Cook an Individual Serving

Prepare a single portion of egg noodles. In the meantime, heat 1
tablespoon of the butter in a small skillet or a wok over medium-
high heat. When the bubbling subsides, add ⅓ cup of the onion and
sauté for about 2 minutes, or until the onion is somewhat limp and
stringy. Add 1⅓ cups of the mushrooms and stir-fry for about 2
minutes, or until they look half-cooked and not quite limp. Scrape
the contents of the skillet into a small bowl.

Measure 1 scant cup of the sliced steak in the skillet and stir-fry
for 2 to 3 minutes; cook the steak only until it is pinkish-rare, since

it will continue to cook on its own. Scrape the meat into the bowl with the mushrooms.

Shake the contents of the jar until smooth; measure out ¼ cup and pour it into the empty skillet. Cook this sauce until thickened and the wine's alcohol has boiled off. Stir the bowl of beef and mushrooms into the skillet and let the ingredients heat through, then serve over a bed of drained noodles.

To Cook Multiple Servings

Cook following the directions above, using a larger skillet and multiplying the portions accordingly.

Lemon-Ginger Shrimp with Pea Pods

Serves 4
Cooking Time: 3 minutes

1 ½ to 2 pounds raw shrimp, shelled and deveined or thawed and drained, if frozen
6 tablespoons cornstarch
1 teaspoon ground ginger
½ teaspoon salt
6 tablespoons corn oil

⅓ cup strained fresh lemon juice
⅓ cup water
1 scallion
2 6-ounce boxes frozen pea pods or ¾ pound fresh snow peas

Drain shrimp of any excess water in a strainer or colander. In a medium-size mixing bowl, combine the cornstarch, ginger, salt, 2 tablespoons of the corn oil, lemon juice, and water; stir well and then mix in the drained shrimp. Chop the scallion 2 inches into the green to get 1 tablespoon; mix this into the shrimp. Cover the bowl with plastic wrap or aluminum foil and refrigerate until ready to use —for up to 1 day.

If you are using frozen pea pods, let them thaw in their packaging; then refrigerate them until needed. If you are using fresh pea pods, let them steep in cold water for 30 minutes so they become crisp. Bring 2 quarts of water to a rolling boil and add the pea pods; let them boil for only 1 minute. Drain immediately and place them in very cold water to cover; once they are cool, drain well, cover, and refrigerate until ready to use.

To Cook an Individual Serving

Heat 1 tablespoon of the oil in a small skillet over medium-high heat. Stir the shrimp mixture in its own container; then, using a slotted spoon, measure out ½ cup of drained shrimp. When a drop of water flicked into the oil in the skillet sizzles, add the shrimp and stir-fry for 1 minute; add ½ box of pea pods (or about one fourth of the fresh pea pods) and continue to stir-fry for another minute. Serve immediately.

To Cook Multiple Servings

Cook following the directions above, multiplying the portions accordingly and using either a wok or a larger skillet. If cooking 3 or 4 servings at once, reduce the oil by ½ or 1 tablespoon respectively.

❧ 7 ❧

DINNERS ON HOLD

These made-in-advance meals-in-one will wait on your stovetop. They can be reheated repeatedly for up to 3 hours without losing quality or flavor.

Chicken Broth with Turkey, Spinach, and Pasta

Chicken and Chick-Peas in a Lemon and Spiced Broth

Tuscan White Bean Soup with Chicken and Orzo

Garden-Fresh Pea Soup with Prosciutto

Corn and Kielbasa Chowder

Beef, Mushroom, and Barley Potage

Chili with Tender Shredded Steak and Pinto Beans

Lentil and Sausage Stew

Onion Soup, Many Ways

Chicken Broth with Turkey, Spinach, and Pasta

Serves 4
Cooking Time: 10 minutes

4 13¾-ounce cans regular-
  strength chicken broth
1 large egg, lightly beaten
½ teaspoon dry dill
Salt to taste
1 pound ground raw turkey,
  fresh or frozen and thawed

1 cup acini pepe pasta
2½ ounces fresh spinach leaves
  (about one fourth of a 10-
  ounce package)
1 lemon

Bring the chicken broth to a boil in a large pot. In the meantime,
combine the egg, dill, salt, ground turkey, and pasta in a mixing
bowl. Wash, dry, and remove the stems from the spinach leaves; use
a pair of scissors to chop the leaves coarsely; place them in a measuring cup and use the scissors to finely mince the spinach until there
is about ¾ cup. Mix the minced spinach into the turkey mixture.

Form a bit of the turkey mixture into a small, bite-size ball, about
1 inch in diameter; drop the ball into the boiling broth; repeat this
procedure using all of the turkey mixture while maintaining the broth
at a gentle boil. When the last ball is dropped in, squeeze the juice
of 1 lemon into the broth; cover and simmer gently for 15 minutes,
or until the pasta is tender. Either serve immediately or let it cool,
uncovered, to room temperature; then cover and refrigerate until
ready to use—for up to 1½ days.

To Cook

Bring the soup to a boil; then lower the heat and simmer, covered,
for 5 to 10 minutes, or until a meatball tests hot at the center. Serve
the desired portion(s).

Keep the pot on the stove, but off the heat, until the time comes
for the next serving; then bring the soup to a boil again and simmer
for 2 to 3 minutes, or until it is heated through. If the temperature
in your house is above 82 degrees, refrigerate the pot between serving times.

Chicken and Chick-Peas in a Lemon and Spiced Broth

Serves 4
Cooking Time: 10 minutes

6 chicken thighs (about 2
 pounds total weight), or 1
 pound boneless chicken
 thighs
1 tablespoon butter
1 tablespoon olive oil
1 large garlic clove, smashed
 and finely minced
1 medium-size onion, chopped
3 tablespoons all-purpose flour
2 13¾-ounce cans regular-
 strength chicken broth (3½
 cups)

1 8-ounce can tomato sauce
1 19-ounce can chick-peas
 (garbanzo beans), drained
1 teaspoon finely chopped
 lemon rind
⅛ teaspoon ground nutmeg
Dash of ground allspice
Scant dash of ground
 cinnamon
Pepper to taste
1 loaf unsliced crusty bread

Remove and discard the skin and bones from the chicken. Use a
heavy mallet or the bottom of a heavy skillet to smash the chicken
almost into shreds; cut the smashed meat into 1- to 2-inch pieces;
set them aside.

Heat the butter and oil in a large soup pot over medium-high
heat. All at once, add the chicken pieces, garlic, and onion; sauté
on all sides until no more pink remains in the chicken. Sprinkle the
flour over the chicken mixture and stir until it has been absorbed;
then stir in the chicken broth, tomato sauce, chick-peas, lemon rind,
spices, and pepper. Bring the mixture to a boil, lower the heat, and
simmer, uncovered, for 10 to 15 minutes. Either serve immediately
with chunks of warm crusty bread or let it cool, uncovered, to room
temperature; then cover and refrigerate until ready to use—for up to
3 days.

To Cook

Bring the cold pot of soup to a boil; then lower the heat and simmer,
uncovered, for about 5 minutes, or until the chicken pieces are hot.
Serve the desired portion(s) along with chunks of warm crusty bread.

Keep the pot on the stove, but off the heat, until the time comes for the next serving; then bring it to a boil again and simmer for a few minutes, until the soup is heated through. If the temperature in your house is above 82 degrees, refrigerate the pot between serving times.

Tuscan White Bean Soup with Chicken and Orzo

Serves 4
Cooking Time: 10 minutes

3 tablespoons bacon drippings
¾ cup peeled and chopped
  celery
¾ cup chopped onion
1 large garlic clove, smashed
  and finely minced
2 15- or 16-ounce cans Great
  Northern white beans or
  shelled beans or pinto beans
3 cups regular-strength canned
  chicken broth

1 16-ounce can whole
  tomatoes
¾ cup diced cooked chicken,
  or 1 5-ounce can "Mixin'
  Chicken"
⅓ cup minced fresh parsley
  leaves, or 1 tablespoon dried
  parsley flakes
⅓ cup orzo macaroni

Heat the bacon drippings in a soup pot over medium-high heat until sizzling. Add the celery to the pot and sauté for several minutes, or until the celery is softened. Add the onion and garlic and sauté the vegetables for several minutes more, or until the onion and celery are limp but not yet browned. Drain the liquid from 1 can of the beans and add the beans to the pot. Mash the beans thoroughly with a potato masher. When the beans are smooth and beginning to bubble, drain the second can of beans and stir them into the pot, along with the chicken broth.

Put the contents of the can of tomatoes in a bowl and use your hands to squish them thoroughly; then stir them into the soup. Add the chicken and parsley; bring to a gentle boil then stir in the orzo. Bring the soup to a boil, lower the heat, and simmer, uncovered, for 20 minutes, or until the orzo is tender; stir from time to time. Either serve the soup immediately or let it cool, uncovered, to room temperature; then cover and refrigerate until ready to use—for up to 3 days.

To Cook

Bring the uncovered cold soup to a boil; then lower the heat and simmer, covered, for about 5 minutes, or until the soup is heated through.

Keep the pot of soup on the stove, but off the heat, until the time comes for the next serving; then bring it to a boil again and simmer for 1 to 2 minutes, or until it is heated through. If the temperature in your home is above 82 degrees, refrigerate the pot between serving times.

Garden-Fresh Pea Soup with Prosciutto

Serves 4
Cooking Time: 10 minutes

2 10-ounce packages frozen peas
2 tablespoons butter
2 tablespoons finely chopped onion
6 ounces prosciutto or boiled ham, cut into julienne matchsticks (about 1¼ cups)
2 tablespoons all-purpose flour
1 cup coarsely chopped lettuce leaves
1 teaspoon sugar
¼ cup minced fresh parsley leaves
1 13¾-ounce can regular-strength chicken broth
1 cup light cream or half-and-half

Unwrap only 1 package of peas; put the block in a mixing bowl, cover with very hot tap water, and set it aside. Melt the butter in a soup pot over medium-high heat. When the bubbling subsides, add the onion and ham; stir and sauté until the onion becomes limp but not yet brown. Remove the pot from the heat and stir in the flour until it has been absorbed; set the pot aside.

Drain the now-thawed peas in a colander; put them in a blender container with the lettuce, sugar, parsley, and chicken broth. Whirl, first at low speed and then at high speed, for 1 minute, or until the ingredients are completely smooth. Pour the purée into the pot containing the ham; stir to blend and combine the flour. Stir in the cream.

Put the remaining, unwrapped package of frozen peas in a mixing bowl, cover with very hot tap water, and allow to thaw for several minutes, then drain the peas and add them to the soup. Set the soup pot over medium heat and wait patiently for it to come to a boil, stirring from the bottom from time to time. When the soup bubbles, let it do so for 1 minute; then remove it from the heat. Either serve the soup immediately or let it cool, uncovered, to room temperature; then cover and refrigerate until ready to use—for up to 3 days.

To Cook

Bring the uncovered cold soup to a boil over medium heat; then lower the heat and simmer, covered, for about 5 minutes, or until the soup is heated through.

Keep the soup pot on the stove, but off the heat, until the time comes for the next serving; then bring the soup to a boil again and simmer for a minute, or until heated through. If the temperature in your home is above 82 degrees, refrigerate the soup between serving times.

Corn and Kielbasa Chowder

Serves 4
Cooking Time: 5 minutes

4 tablespoons butter
¾ pound smoked kielbasa, cut
  into thin rounds
1 medium-size onion, finely
  chopped
2 13¾-ounce cans regular-
  strength chicken broth

1 cup mashed potato flakes
½ cup milk
2 10-ounce packages frozen
  corn

Melt the butter in a soup pot over medium-high heat. When the bubbling subsides, add the kielbasa and onion; stir and sauté for about 5 minutes, or until the kielbasa rounds become rosy and begin to pucker slightly. Add the remaining ingredients and heat slowly, until the corn thaws and the potato flakes dissolve to smoothness. Let the chowder simmer for 1 minute and remove the pot from the heat. Either serve the chowder immediately or let it cool, uncovered, to room temperature; then cover and refrigerate until ready to use—for up to 3 days.

To Cook

Bring the uncovered cold chowder to a boil over medium-high heat; then lower the heat and simmer, covered, for 2 to 3 minutes, or until it is heated through.

Keep the pot on the stove, but off the heat, until the time comes for the next serving; then bring the chowder to a boil again and simmer for a minute or two, or until it is heated through. If the temperature in your home is above 82 degrees, refrigerate the chowder between serving times.

Beef, Mushroom, and Barley Potage

Serves 4
Cooking Time: 5 to 10 minutes

4 13¾-ounce cans regular-
  strength beef broth
1 cup pearl barley or brown
  rice (Don't use unpearled or
  quick barley.)
9 tablespoons butter
12 ounces fresh mushrooms,
  coarsely sliced

1½ pounds boneless chuck
  steak
1 teaspoon salt
Pepper to taste
1 tablespoon Worchestershire
  sauce

Bring 3 of the cans of beef broth to a boil in a soup pot and stir in the barley; return to a boil then cover, lower the heat, and simmer for either 30 minutes or 1 hour, following the directions on the package.

In the meantime, heat 6 tablespoons of the butter in a skillet over medium-high heat. When the bubbling subsides, add the coarsely sliced mushrooms; stir and sauté for several minutes, or until the mushrooms are limp and cooked. Remove the mushrooms from the heat and allow them to cool slightly. Spoon the mushrooms into a blender or food processor container; pour in the remaining can of beef broth and whirl at high speed until smoothly puréed; set aside.

Trim the fat from the chuck steak; then cut the meat very thinly, across the grain and on a diagonal, into small shred-like pieces. Heat the remaining 3 tablespoons of butter in a skillet over medium-high heat. When the bubbling subsides, add the sliced meat and stir and sauté until the meat is just medium-rare. Remove the skillet from the heat and stir in the salt, pepper, and Worchestershire sauce; stir to coat the meat and then set the skillet aside.

When the barley is cooked, stir the mushroom purée and the seasoned meat into it. Let the potage cool, uncovered, to room temperature; then cover and refrigerate until ready to use—for up to 2 days.

To Cook

Bring the uncovered cold potage to a gentle boil; then lower the heat and simmer, covered, for about 5 minutes, or until the soup is heated through.

Keep the soup on the stove, but off the heat, until the time comes for the next serving; then bring the soup to a boil again and simmer it for 1 to 2 minutes, or until it is heated through. If the temperature in your home is above 82 degrees, refrigerate the pot between serving times.

Chili with Tender Shredded Steak and Pinto Beans

Serves 4
Cooking Time: 10 to 15 minutes

1½ pounds boneless chuck
  steak
6 tablespoons bacon drippings
  or olive oil
2 cups chopped onion
3 large garlic cloves, smashed
  and finely minced
3 tablespoons chili powder
1 teaspoon salt
½ teaspoon ground cumin
¼ teaspoon cayenne pepper

4 dashes of ground allspice
2 16-ounce cans tomatoes (1
  quart, if using home-canned
  tomatoes)
3 tablespoons tomato paste
2 16-ounce cans pinto beans
1 13¾-ounce can regular-
  strength beef broth
1 cup water
1 loaf unsliced crusty bread

Trim the fat from the meat; then cut the meat very thinly, across the grain and on a diagonal, into small shred-like slices. Set the shredded meat aside.

Melt the bacon drippings over high heat in a large soup pot; when a drop of water flicked into the fat sizzles, add the onion and the garlic; stir and sauté for 1 minute, or until the onion softens. Add the meat and sauté, stirring, until it is medium-rare. Remove the pot from the heat and add the chili powder, salt, cumin, cayenne pepper, and allspice; stir to coat the meat and set the pot aside.

Pour the canned tomatoes into a mixing bowl; use your hand to squish the tomatoes into small pieces. Stir the tomato paste into the tomatoes and add the 2 undrained cans of beans. Pour this tomato-bean mixture into the pot of meat and stir in the beef broth and water. Bring the mixture to a boil; then lower the heat and simmer, uncovered, for 20 minutes. Either serve it immediately or let it cool completely to room temperature; then cover and refrigerate until ready to use—for up to 2 days.

To Cook

Bring the cold chili to a boil over medium-high heat; then lower the heat and simmer, uncovered, for 5 to 10 minutes, or until the chili has thickened to your liking. Serve with hunks of crusty bread.

Keep the pot of chili on the stove, but off the heat, until the time comes for the next serving; then bring the chili to a boil again and simmer it for 1 to 2 minutes, or until it is heated through. If the temperature in your home is above 82 degrees, refrigerate the pot between serving times.

Lentil and Sausage Stew

Serves 4
Cooking Time: 5 to 10 minutes

1 pound dried lentils, about
   2½ cups, sorted and rinsed
2 10½-ounce cans undiluted,
   condensed beef broth or
   consommé
6 cups water
1 pound Italian sweet sausage
1 tablespoon olive oil
1 medium-size onion, chopped

1 6-ounce can tomato paste
3 tablespoons minced fresh
   parsley leaves, or 1
   tablespoon dried parsley
   flakes
1 teaspoon salt
Pepper to taste
1 loaf unsliced crusty bread

Put the lentils into a large pot. Add the beef broth and water and bring to a boil. As the pot heats, cut the sausage into 1- to 1½-inch chunks. When the broth boils, add the sausage chunks; and return to a boil. Cover the pot, lower the heat, and simmer for 30 minutes.

In the meantime, heat the oil in a small skillet over medium-high heat. Add the onion and sauté for about 3 minutes, or until the onion is limp; remove the skillet from the heat and set it aside.

When the lentils and sausages have cooked for 30 minutes, stir in the contents of the skillet; then add the tomato paste, parsley, salt, and pepper. Remove the pot from the heat and let it cool, uncovered, to room temperature. Cover and refrigerate until ready to use —for up to 3 days.

To Cook

Bring the uncovered cold stew to a boil; then cover, lower the heat, and simmer for 5 minutes. Serve with hunks of crusty bread.

Keep the covered pot of stew on the stove, but off the heat, until the time comes for the next serving; then bring the stew to a boil again and simmer it for 1 to 2 minutes, or until it is heated through. If the temperature in your home is above 82 degrees, refrigerate the pot between serving times.

Onion Soup, Many Ways

Serves 4
Cooking Time: 5 to 10 minutes

4 medium-to-large Bermuda,
   Spanish, or yellow onions
   (about 1 ½ pounds total
   weight)
4 tablespoons butter
Pepper to taste
4 tablespoons all-purpose flour

3 13¾-ounce cans regular-
   strength beef broth (5¼
   cups)
6 ounces Monterey Jack, Swiss,
   Bon Bel, mozzarella, or
   Gouda cheese
4 cups plain croutons

Peel the onions, cut each in half; slice each half thinly. Melt the butter in a soup pot over medium heat; when the bubbling subsides, add the onions and pepper and cook, uncovered, stirring often, for 20 to 30 minutes, or until the onions are a golden amber-brown; don't let them burn or get dark brown. Sprinkle the onions with 2 tablespoons of the flour and stir until the flour has been absorbed; then add the beef broth and blend it in. Bring to a boil; then lower the heat and simmer, uncovered, for 10 minutes. Remove the pot from the heat and let it cool to room temperature. Cover and refrigerate until ready to use—for up to 2 days.

While the soup cools, shred the cheese to get 2 to 2½ cups; mix the remaining 2 tablespoons of flour into the cheese shreds to prevent sticking; package in a plastic sandwich bag and refrigerate until ready to use.

To Cook

Bring the cold uncovered soup to a gentle boil; then lower the heat and simmer, covered, for several minutes, or until it is heated through. Set your oven to its broil setting; leave the oven door slightly ajar. Ladle 1½ cups of hot soup into an individual serving-size, ovenproof soup ramekin; cover with a scant cup of croutons and sprinkle with ½ cup of the shredded cheese. Repeat this process for as many servings as you intend to serve right now. Carefully place the assembled ramekin(s) 6 inches away from the broiling element and, briefly, allow the cheese to melt and bubble. Serve immediately.

Keep the pot of soup on the stove, but off the heat, until the time comes for the next serving; then reheat the soup, assemble, and broil as directed above. If the temperature in your home is above 82 degrees, refrigerate the pot between serving times.

Variations:

CREAMY ONION SOUP

Stir ⅓ cup of heavy cream into the soup after the beef broth.

FRENCH-STYLE ONION SOUP

After sprinkling the flour into the cooked onions, stir in 1½ cups of dry white wine; bring to a boil, add only 2 cans of beef broth, and let simmer, uncovered, for 15 minutes.

LEEK SOUP

Replace the onions with 3 or 4 large leeks (about 1½ pounds total weight) sliced thinly. Replace the beef broth with the same amount of chicken broth, plus ¼ cup of milk or heavy or light cream.

ॐ 8 ॐ

READY-MADE
ROOM-TEMPERATURE MEALS

These preassembled, ready-to-eat, complete meals await any dinnertime, winter or summer. They are best when served at room temperature.

Curry-Lime Chicken and Rice Salad

Kielbasa-Potato Salad

Tangy Sausage, Chick-Pea, and Potato Salad

Ham and Cheese Tortilla Rolls

Individual Antipasto Plates

Greek Salad

Spiced Beef and Lettuce Bundles

Other Ideas

Curry-Lime Chicken and Rice Salad

Serves 4
Cooking Time: None

2½ pounds chicken breasts
1 onion, coarsely diced
3 celery stalks, scraped and cut
into chunks
2 carrots, cut into chunks
2 thin lime slices
6 whole black peppercorns
1½ tablespoons butter
¾ cup long-grain converted
rice
¾ teaspoon salt

Pepper to taste
1 13¾-ounce can regular-
strength chicken broth
½ cup mayonnaise
1 tablespoon plus ½ teaspoon
curry powder
⅛ cup strained fresh lime or
lemon juice
2 teaspoons snipped fresh
chives, or 1 to 3 tablespoons
chopped scallions

Put the chicken breasts, skin side down, in an ample pot and add the onion, celery, carrots, lime slices, and peppercorns; pour 2 inches of water into the pot. Put the pot over high heat, cover, and bring to a boil; then lower the heat and simmer for 15 to 20 minutes, or until a knife slash at the thickest part of the breast shows the meat to be cooked to the bone. Transfer the breasts to a dinner plate to cool while you make the pilaf.

Melt the butter in a heavy saucepan over medium heat. When it bubbles, stir in the rice, ½ teaspoon of the salt, and pepper; sauté, stirring frequently, until the rice takes on a slightly translucent quality (don't let the kernels get brown or pop). Slowly stir in the chicken broth (if your can of broth contains 14½ ounces, add 1 more tablespoon of rice to the pot); bring to a boil over high heat; then cover and lower the heat to maintain a steady simmer for 20 to 25 minutes, or until nearly all the liquid has been absorbed. Turn off the heat and let stand, without removing the cover, for 10 minutes. Remove the cover and spread the rice, uncovered, on 2 dinner plates to cool.

While the rice cooks, combine the mayonnaise and 1 tablespoon of the curry powder in a small bowl; set it aside. When the chicken is cool enough to handle, remove and discard the skin and bones; shred the meat into bite-size pieces and put them in a medium-size mixing bowl. Combine the lime juice, the ½ teaspoon of curry, and

¼ teaspoon of salt; drizzle the mixture over the chicken in the bowl and toss well so that all the chicken pieces absorb the juice; let stand for 10 minutes.

Put the cooled rice in a large mixing bowl and stir in the curried mayonnaise and the chicken. Divide the completed salad among 4 shallow bowls or onto 4 dinner plates lined with lettuce. Sprinkle each portion with ½ teaspoon of snipped chives or 1 to 2 teaspoons of chopped scallions. Cover with plastic wrap or aluminum foil and refrigerate until ready to use—for up to 3 days.

To Serve

Allow the portions to come to room temperature before serving.

Kielbasa-Potato Salad

Serves 4
Cooking Time: None

4 medium-size potatoes,
  peeled
⅓ cup distilled white vinegar
½ teaspoon sugar
½ teaspoon salt
¼ teaspoon dry mustard
⅛ teaspoon paprika

2 tablespoons butter
¼ cup chopped onion
¼ cup chopped scraped celery
⅓ cup mayonnaise
1 pound precooked kielbasa
  sausage

Boil the potatoes in a large pot of water for 20 to 25 minutes. In the meantime, combine the vinegar, sugar, salt, mustard, and paprika in a small mixing bowl; set it aside. Melt the butter in a frying pan over medium-high heat. Add the onion and celery and sauté until the vegetables are limp. Pour in the vinegar mixture and bring to a boil; then lower the heat and simmer for 1 minute. Pour the mixture back into the small mixing bowl and set it aside, uncovered, to cool.

Test the potatoes to see if they are done by poking the largest one with a pointed knife; when the center offers no resistance, drain off all the cooking water and replace it with cold water; let the potatoes sit in this water for 10 minutes. In the meantime, blend the mayonnaise into the bowl of vinegar dressing. Cut the potatoes into ½-inch dice and put them in a large mixing bowl. Pour the dressing over the potatoes and stir to coat each piece with the dressing; then set aside.

Cut the kielbasa into thin slices and sauté them in a frying pan over medium-high heat for 10 to 15 minutes, stirring frequently. When the fat has been rendered out of the kielbasa slices and they are slightly browned, use a slotted spoon to transfer them to the bowl of potatoes; discard the rendered fat. Stir the mixture together and divide it equally among 4 shallow soup bowls; cover with plastic wrap or aluminum foil and refrigerate until ready to use—for up to 3 days.

To Serve

Allow the portions to come to room temperature before serving.

Tangy Sausage, Chick-Pea, and Potato Salad

Serves 4
Cooking Time: None

1 pound Italian sweet sausages
4 medium-size potatoes,
  peeled
⅓ cup strained fresh lemon
  juice
3 tablespoons olive oil
3 tablespoons corn oil
1 small onion, coarsely
  chopped

1 teaspoon salt
2 tablespoons snipped fresh
  parsley leaves (Don't use
  dried parsley flakes.)
1 16- or 19-ounce can chick-
  peas (garbanzo beans)

Bring a large pot of water to a boil over high heat; use a knife-tip to prick the sausages twice on each side; put the sausages in the pot and boil for 10 minutes. After 10 minutes, drop in the peeled potatoes and return to a boil; cook the combined ingredients for 20 minutes.

In the meantime, combine the lemon juice, olive and corn oils, onion, and salt in a blender container; whirl at high speed until the onion is liquefied; then stir in the parsley by hand and set the dressing aside. Rinse the chick-peas repeatedly in a colander to remove all the starchy can liquid; then drain well.

When the sausages are cooked, transfer them to a dinner plate to cool, uncovered. Test the potatoes to see if they are done by poking the largest one with a pointed knife; when the center offers no resistance, drain off all the cooking water and replace it with cold water; let the potatoes sit in this water for 10 minutes.

When the potatoes are cool enough to handle, cut them into ½-inch dice and put them in a large mixing bowl. Add the drained chick-peas, drizzle all the dressing over this mixture; then stir with your fingers to coat each piece. Cover with plastic wrap or aluminum foil and set aside at room temperature for 1 hour. Cover and refrigerate the sausages.

After the hour, gently toss the potato and chick-pea mixture and divide it equally among 4 shallow soup bowls. Cut the sausages into ¼-inch-thick slices and distribute equal amounts on top of each bowl without mixing them in. Cover each bowl with plastic wrap or aluminum foil and refrigerate until ready to use—for up to 2 days.

To Serve

Allow the portions to come to room temperature; toss gently just before serving.

Ham and Cheese Tortilla Rolls

Serves 4
Cooking Time: None

8 ounces (8 slices) boiled ham
1 12-ounce container sharp
    Cheddar cold-pack cheese
    food, at room temperature

8 8-inch-diameter flour
    tortillas, at room
    temperature
1 ounce alfalfa sprouts

Chop the ham and separate it into 8 equal piles. Spread 2 table-spoons of the softened cheese over 1 tortilla, leaving a ½-inch margin all around. Spread 1 pile of chopped ham over the cheese; sprinkle just a small pinch or two of sprouts on top of the cheese. Roll up the tortilla tightly, jelly roll fashion; then wrap snugly in plastic wrap. Repeat this process with the remaining ingredients. Refrigerate until ready to use—for up to 2 days.

To Serve

Serve at room temperature or chilled.

Individual Antipasto Plates

Serves 4
Cooking Time: None

Lettuce
8 slices Genoa salami (about 2
  ounces total weight)
4 slices Provolone cheese
  (about 1 ounce total weight)
4 slices boiled him (about 4
  ounces total weight)
1 cucumber, peeled, seeded,
  and cut into sticks
Tuna Spread (recipe follows)
1 loaf crusty Italian bread
4 inner celery stalks, leaves
  removed
1 tomato, quartered and
  sprinkled with salt

Your choice of two or more of
  the following:
8 green and/or black olives,
  any kind
8 slices pepperoni
4 slices Kasseri or Italian
  table cheese
1 6-ounce jar marinated
  artichoke hearts, drained
4 to 8 anchovy fillets
4 to 8 pimiento slices
4 to 8 hot Italian or Greek
  Salonika peppers
2 hard-boiled eggs,
  quartered
Bottled marinated eggplant
  pieces, drained
Marinated Mushrooms
  (recipe follows)

Line 4 dinner plates with lettuce leaves. Cut the salami and Provolone into quarters and arrange the triangles equally around the rim of each plate. Roll up the ham slices around the cucumber sticks and cut them in half; place equal portions at the center of each plate.

Make the Tuna Spread and spread it on 4 generous slices of Italian bread; place a slice on each plate along with equal portions of the celery and tomato. Add to each plate 2 or more items from the remaining ingredients list. Cover each plate with plastic wrap or aluminum foil and refrigerate until ready to use—for up to 2 days.

Tuna Spread

8 tablespoons (1 stick) butter
1/4 cup strained fresh lemon
   juice
1 small onion, coarsely
   chopped (about 1/8 to 1/4
   cup)

Scant 1/4 teaspoon Tabasco
   sauce
1/8 teaspoon salt
Pepper to taste
1 6 1/2-ounce can tuna in oil

Melt the butter in a small saucepan; then pour it into a small bowl and allow it to cool to room temperature. Put the lemon juice, onion, Tabasco sauce, salt, and pepper in a blender container and whirl at high speed until liquefied. Drain the oil from the tuna and discard it; add half the tuna to the blender and whirl until smooth. With the blender still running, bit by bit, add the remaining tuna until smooth. Blend in the cooled butter in a steady stream. When smooth, stop the blender and pour the mixture into a pretty jar, crock, or ramekin. Cover and refrigerate for 1 hour before using.

Marinated Mushrooms

16 ounces fresh mushrooms
3/4 cup corn oil
1/4 cup olive oil
1/2 cup strained fresh lemon
   juice
1 small onion, coarsely
   chopped

1 tablespoon snipped fresh
   parsley leaves, or 1 teaspoon
   dried parsley flakes
1 teaspoon salt
1/4 teaspoon pepper

Bring a pot of water to a rolling boil; remove and discard mushroom stems. Add the mushroom caps to the pot, cover, and simmer for 8 to 10 minutes, or until no white remains; drain in a strainer. Whirl the remaining ingredients in a blender at high speed until liquefied. Put the drained mushrooms in a jar or plastic container and pour in the marinade from the blender. Stir to coat the mushrooms; cover and let stand at room temperature for 6 hours. Refrigerate until ready to use—for up to 2 weeks, shaking the jar from day to day.

To use, shake the jar then drain the mushrooms in a strainer. Gently roll the mushrooms between paper towels to remove any excess marinade.

Greek Salad

Serves 4
Serving Time: 3 to 5 minutes

FETA-OREGANO DRESSING
3 tablespoons olive oil
3 tablespoons corn oil
2 tablespoons strained fresh
  lemon juice
2 tablespoons red wine vinegar
1 small garlic clove, smashed
  and very finely minced
1 ½ teaspoons dried oregano,
  rubbed to a powder between
  the heels of your hands
Scant ¼ teaspoon salt
⅛ teaspoon pepper
8 ounces feta cheese

Your choice of dressing
1 head iceberg lettuce
1 cucumber, peeled and sliced
1 ripe tomato, cut up
½ sweet green pepper, cut into
  strips
3 radishes, cut into thin slices
1 scallion, chopped, optional

FETA-DILL DRESSING
3 tablespoons olive oil
3 tablespoons corn oil
2 tablespoons strained fresh
  lemon juice
2 tablespoons distilled white
  vinegar
1 tablespoon snipped fresh
  dillweed, or 1 teaspoon
  dried dill
Scant ¼ teaspoon salt
8 ounces feta cheese

12 or more Calamata Greek
  olives
8 Salonika hot green peppers,
  optional
8 anchovy fillets, optional
1 loaf fresh crusty Italian or
  French bread

Make your choice of dressing: Combine the 2 oils in a medium-size mixing bowl; whisk in the lemon juice and vinegar until blended and smooth. Add all the remaining ingredients, except the feta cheese. Use your fingertips to crumble the feta cheese into the smallest possible bits; stir these bits into the dressing so that all the pieces are coated. Cover the dressing and refrigerate until ready to use.

Tear the lettuce into chunks and divide it equally among 4 serving bowls ample enough to allow tossing room. Put equal portions of the cucumber, tomato, green pepper, radishes, scallion, olives, and hot peppers in each bowl; toss to mix. Top each bowl with a criss-cross of anchovy fillets; cover and refrigerate until ready to use—for up to 1 ½ days.

To Serve

Break the bread into fist-size chunks. Put them in a bread basket, cover with a napkin, and set the basket on your dining table.

Stir the dressing before spooning the desired amount over each single portion; toss well and then serve the salads accompanied by the bread.

Spiced Beef and Lettuce Bundles

Serves 4
Cooking Time: None

ORIENTAL MARINADE

3 tablespoons soy sauce
1 tablespoon sugar
1 garlic clove, smashed and
    finely minced
1/4 teaspoon ground ginger
3 tablespoons chopped
    scallions

Your choice of marinade
1 1/4 to 1 1/2 pounds lean,
    boneless steak, such as beef
    round sirloin, top round, or
    chuck
2 tablespoons corn oil
1 1/4 cups regular-strength
    canned beef broth

HOT AND TANGY MARINADE

1/3 cup strained fresh lime juice
3 tablespoons soy sauce
1/2 teaspoon cayenne powder
3 tablespoons chopped
    scallions
1 cucumber

1/2 cup long-grain converted
    rice
2 large, unused (whole) heads
    lettuce

Toothpicks

Make your choice of either marinade by combining the ingredients in a cup or bowl. If you are making the Hot and Tangy Marinade, peel the cucumber, cut off the tips and cut away lengths of just the cucumber flesh, leaving and discarding the seed core; cut the seedless portion of the cucumber into 1-inch-long matchsticks; stir them into the marinade. Set either marinade aside.

Use your sharpest knife to remove any excess fat from the meat; then cut the meat across the grain and on the diagonal into strips 1/8 inch or thinner by 1 to 2 inches. Heat the oil in a non-stick skillet over medium-high heat; add the meat strips and sauté stirring and turning. When too much meat liquid has exuded and the meat begins to boil instead of sautéing, immediately drain it off before continuing. Cook until the meat is just tender and some rosiness still remains. Thoroughly drain off all the pan juices and put the meat into a mixing bowl; pour your choice of prepared marinade over the meat and toss to coat all the pieces. Allow to cool, uncovered, stirring the mixture now and then. Once cool, cover and refrigerate for either 2 hours or overnight.

While the meat marinates, prepare the rice: Bring the broth to a boil in a saucepan; stir in the rice, cover, and simmer for 20 minutes. Turn off the heat and let the rice stand without removing the cover for 10 minutes. Uncover the rice; transfer it to 2 dinner plates to prevent further cooking and allow it to cool; cover and refrigerate for as long as the meat marinates.

To assemble, wash, drain, and remove the cores from both heads of lettuce; use paper towels to absorb any excess water. Remove the first outer leaf of lettuce, being careful not to rip it; cut off an inch or two of the thick leaf-stem. Put about 8 to 10 pieces of marinated meat at the bottom, thick part of the leaf; top the meat with 1 or 2 rounded tablespoons of rice; roll up the leaf, tucking in the sides as you do; pierce the roll with several toothpicks at a slant to secure it; place the bundle on a paper towel-lined serving platter. Repeat this process for the rest of the meat; use the second head of lettuce when the leaves become too small to handle. Cover the platter and refrigerate until ready to use—for up to 2 days.

To Serve

Serve at room temperature, using 2 rolls for each person. Hold the bundles in your hands to eat.

If you won't be home to serve the meal, leave a warning note about the toothpicks.

OTHER IDEAS

Everyone has his or her own favorite recipes for the following ready-made room-temperature meals. This list can serve as a reminder.

Cold Fried Chicken

Use either your own homemade or frozen-and-cooked fried chicken pieces; refrigerate along with the ready-made Spiral Pasta Salad on page 217. Serve at room temperature or else chilled.

Taco Salad

Prepare a hearty, ready-made salad-meal in 4 separate portions, using lettuce, tomatoes, scallions, shredded Cheddar cheese, and nacho chips broken into bite-size pieces; cover each portion and refrigerate. To serve, drizzle bottled taco or sour cream salad dressing over each portion as needed.

Hearty Potato Salad

Make your favorite potato salad recipe and add to it your choice or all of the following: cubed ham, chopped hard-boiled eggs, and/or cooked and crumbled bacon. Cover and refrigerate. Serve at room temperature.

Tuna-Mac Salad

Prepare a salad of canned tuna, cooked macaroni, and chopped celery (cooked peas are optional) held together by mayonnaise. Refrigerate until serving time. Cooked chicken can be substituted for the tuna.

Ham or Beef Rolls

Wrap thin slices of cold cooked ham around ½-inch-wide sticks of honeydew melon or wrap thin slices of cold cooked, lightly-salted-and-peppered roast beef around ½-inch-wide sticks (seeds removed) of cucumber; arrange on plates. Also, make any of the ready-made side dishes from Chapter 11 (pages 211–21) as an accompaniment. Cover and refrigerate. Serve at room temperature.

Chef's Salad

Prepare 4 separate portions of chef's salad using lettuce, cucumbers, tomatoes, green peppers, plus your choice of or all of the following: ham or roast beef or salami in julienne strips, shredded cooked chicken, crab meat, cooked shrimp, tuna, shredded or cubed cheese, chick-peas, alfalfa sprouts, chopped hard-boiled eggs, raw sliced mushrooms, bacon bits, radishes, carrot curls, and/or olives. Cover each portion and refrigerate.

To serve, drizzle your choice of bottled salad dressing over each portion as needed. Serve with hunks of crusty Italian bread.

❦ 9 ❧

HOT SUPPER SANDWICHES

Here are some hearty, restaurant-quality sandwiches that can be served in minutes.

Shaved Roast Beef for Sandwiches

Roast Beef and Boursin

Roast Beef Heros—Four Kinds

French Dip

Open-Faced Roast Beef with Gravy

Roast Beef with Cheddar Sauce

Ready-Made Lone Star Burritos

Bayou Beef Buns

Souvlakia

Chicken Salad Burgers

Sausage Heros

Ready-Made Ham and Cheese Buns

Grilled Cheese Tortillas

Skewered Mozzarella Loaves

Steamed Corned Beef on Rye

Shaved Roast Beef for Sandwiches

Makes enough for 8 sandwiches

4¼ pounds boneless eye round   8 zip-lock sandwich bags
    beef

Preheat the oven to 325 degrees. Put the beef, straight from the refrigerator, into a pan with the fat side up; no rack is necessary. Roast for 1 hour and 5 minutes, or the equivalent of 15 minutes per pound. This is not the usual cooking time for medium-rare roast beef, but the time applies to this particular recipe because you will not be immediately slicing the hot roast beef: instead, it will continue to cook from its own inner heat as it cools.

Transfer the cooked roast beef from its pan to a dinner plate and allow it to cool, unsliced and uncovered, for several hours, or until it is room temperature. When it is no longer warm, wrap the roast snugly in aluminum foil and refrigerate it overnight.

Cut off and discard all the fat and grizzled skin from the cold roast beef. Begin shaving the beef at one tip, across the grain, cutting the thinnest possible shaved slices alternately from the edges. Rather than cutting off a whole slice of beef, you will shave off pieces only 1 or 2 inches wide. Continue shaving the meat from the edges and also from the center in strips, until the whole roast has been shaved. You will note that the meat is rare to medium-rare. This is to compensate for the further cooking it will get when it is used in the recipes that follow.

Put 1 cup of shaved meat into each of the 8 sandwich bags. You may want to refrigerate 4 of the bags for use in the next 2 days and freeze the other 4 bags for another time. Each 1-cup portion in each bag will make one of the roast beef sandwiches from this chapter.

To Make the French Dip recipe on page 174

After transferring the just-cooked roast beef to a dinner plate to cool, pour 1 13¾-ounce can of regular-strength beef broth into the pan of hot beef drippings; set it aside while the roast cools. Pour any extra drippings from the cooling roast into the broth; sprinkle the broth with pepper to taste. If the weather is hot, refrigerate the pan to hasten the fat congealing on top.

Measure 2 teaspoons of cornstarch into a 3-cup jar. Scrape the bottom of the pan to loosen all the drippings. Strain the pan's contents into the jar of cornstarch so as to remove the fat. Cover and then shake the jar to dissolve the cornstarch; label and refrigerate until ready to use—for up to 4 days.

To Make the Open-Faced Roast Beef with Gravy
recipe on page 175

Follow the preceding French Dip directions, using 1 13¾-ounce can regular-strength beef broth and replacing the cornstarch with 3½ tablespoons of flour. Once these ingredients are in the jar, add ½ teaspoon Kitchen Bouquet or Gravy Master before shaking and refrigerating.

Roast Beef and Boursin

Serves 4
Cooking Time: 5 minutes

4 10- or 11-inch-long skinny hero rolls, or 8 small hero or torpedo rolls each about 5 inches long
4 tablespoons butter, melted

8 ounces Boursin or any other French-style, Neufchâtel cheese with herbs and garlic, softened
4 cups Shaved Roast Beef (page 169)
Salt to taste

Split the rolls open lengthwise; spread on your work surface, cut sides up. Brush only one cut side of each roll with 1 tablespoon of melted butter. (If you are using the 8 smaller rolls, halve these amounts accordingly.) Spread 2 ounces of the softened cheese over *each* of the other cut sides. Lay 1 cup of beef slices over each of the buttered sides; sprinkle with salt, if you wish. Transfer the sandwiches, still open, to 1 big rimmed baking sheet or between several smaller ones, depending on your individual and multiple cooking plans. Cover with plastic wrap and refrigerate until ready to use—for up to 1½ days.

To Cook

Preheat the oven to 425 degrees. Discard the plastic wrap and set the open sandwich(es) in their pan on the middle rack of the oven. Bake for 5 minutes, or until the cheese is well softened; remove from the oven and fold the 2 halves together into a sandwich. Cut the long roll in half and serve warm.

Roast Beef Heros — Four Kinds

Serves 4
Cooking Time: 3 minutes

4 tablespoons butter
4 cups Shaved Roast Beef
    (page 169)
Salt and pepper to taste

4 10- or 11-inch-long skinny
    hero rolls, or 8 small 5-inch-
    long hero or torpedo rolls
Your choice of filling (recipes
    follow)

To Cook an Individual Serving

Heat 1 tablespoon of the butter in a skillet over medium-high heat.
When the bubbling subsides, add 1 cup of shaved roast beef plus salt
and lots of pepper to taste. Stir to coat the meat in the butter; when
the butter resumes its bubbling, add 1 portion of your choice of
filling and sauté and stir it with the beef for not quite a minute, or
until all the ingredients are heated through (in the case of the cheese
filling, until it is melted). Spread the mixture into split roll(s); cut
the long skinny roll in half and serve.

To Cook Multiple Servings

Cook following the directions above, multiplying the portions accordingly.

Philadelphia Cheese Steak

½ pound Monterey Jack
    cheese
4 teaspoons all-purpose flour

4 zip-lock sandwich bags

Shred the cheese and sprinkle in the flour to coat it. Divide the
filling among the sandwich bags. Refrigerate the 4 portions until
ready to use—for up to 4 days.

Roast Beef and Onions

2 medium-size onions   4 zip-lock sandwich bags
3 tablespoons butter

Slice the onions into thin rings. Melt the butter in a skillet over medium heat. Add the onions and sauté and stir for about 10 minutes, or until they are limp but not brown or stringy. Allow to cool and then divide the 4 onion portions among the sandwich bags. Refrigerate until ready to use—for up to 4 days.

Roast Beef and Mushrooms

8 ounces fresh mushrooms   4 zip-lock sandwich bags
4 tablespoons butter

Slice the mushrooms to get 3 to 3½ cups. Melt the butter in a skillet over medium to medium-high heat. When the sizzling subsides, add the mushrooms. Stir and sauté until the mushrooms look just cooked and their juices begin to bubble. Use a slotted spoon to transfer just the mushrooms to a dinner plate to cool. Divide the mushroom portions among the 4 sandwich bags. Refrigerate until ready to use—for up to 4 days.

Roast Beef and Peppers

3 large sweet green peppers   4 zip-lock sandwich bags
4 tablespoons butter

Seed the peppers and cut them into thin strips. Melt the butter in a skillet over medium heat. Add the peppers and sauté and stir for 10 to 15 minutes, or until they are soft but not brown. Allow them to cool. Divide the portions among the 4 sandwich bags. Refrigerate until ready to use—for up to 4 days.

Roast Beef Combination Heros

Make mixtures of any of the filling choices above, by first combining the listed ingredients and then dividing the amount of those ingredients by the number of combinations you have used.

French Dip

Serves 4
Cooking Time: 5 minutes

The jar of beef broth, pan
  drippings, and cornstarch
  from the Shaved Roast Beef
  recipe (pages 169–70)
4 tablespoons butter
4 cups Shaved Roast Beef
  (page 169)

Salt and pepper to taste
4 10- or 11-inch-long skinny
  hero rolls, or 8 small 5-inch-
  long hero or torpedo rolls

To Cook an Individual Serving

Shake the jar of broth and drippings to distribute the cornstarch;
then measure ⅓ cup into a small saucepan; heat and stir over high
heat until boiling and somewhat thickened. Set this au jus gravy
aside over the lowest heat.

    Melt 1 tablespoon of the butter in a skillet over medium-high heat.
When the bubbling subsides, add 1 cup of shaved roast beef plus salt
and lots of pepper to taste. Stir and sauté the beef for not quite a
minute, or until it is hot but not overcooked. Put the beef in split
roll(s); cut the long skinny roll in half. Pour the hot au jus gravy into
a 6-ounce heatproof custard cup; place it on a dinner plate along
with the sandwich. To eat, dip the end of the sandwich into the cup
of gravy before each bite.

To Cook Multiple Servings

Cook following the directions above, multiplying the portions accordingly.

Open-Faced Roast Beef with Gravy

Serves 4
Cooking Time: 5 minutes

4 slices bread
The jar of beef broth, pan
    drippings, and flour from the
    Shaved Roast Beef recipe
    (pages 169–70)

4 cups Shaved Roast Beef
    (page 169)
Salt and pepper to taste

To Cook an Individual Serving

Place a slice of bread on a dinner plate and set it aside. Shake the jar
of broth and drippings to distribute the flour. Measure ½ cup into a
small saucepan; heat and stir over medium-high heat until boiling
and thickened. Turn the heat to medium-low and add a 1-cup portion of shaved beef; simmer for a minute, or until heated through
but not quite bubbling; don't overcook. Quickly stir in salt and
pepper to taste and serve over the bread.

To Cook Multiple Servings

Cook following the directions above, multiplying the portions accordingly.

Roast Beef with Cheddar Sauce

Serves 4
Cooking Time: 10 minutes

1 8-ounce jar Cheez Whiz
4 cups Shaved Roast Beef
   (page 169)
Pepper to taste

4 10- or 11-inch-long skinny
   hero rolls, or 8 small 5-inch-
   long hero or torpedo rolls

To Cook an Individual Serving

Heat ¼ cup (4 tablespoons) of the Cheez Whiz in a small saucepan over medium heat until it is liquid. Add 1 cup of shaved roast beef and stir continuously until all the pieces are coated; sprinkle with pepper to taste. Let the mixture cook for 3 to 5 minutes, or until it is heated through; spread on one side of a split long roll (or between 2 smaller rolls); cover with the matching half and serve.

To Cook Multiple Servings

Cook following the directions above, multiplying the portions accordingly.

Ready-Made Lone Star Burritos

Serves 4
Cooking Time: 10 minutes

Made in advance and individually wrapped, these tender, steak-filled burritos can be baked and served in 10 minutes.

1 teaspoon chili powder
1/2 teaspoon dried oregano
1/2 teaspoon salt
1/4 teaspoon pepper
1 1/2 pounds boneless beef
   chuck steak
8 8-inch-diameter flour tortillas
1 lime

1/2 cup chopped scallions
1 1/2 cups chopped ripe
   tomatoes
1 cup sour cream, optional

8 4- by 6-inch aluminum foil
   rectangles

Preheat the oven to the broil setting, leaving the door slightly ajar. Combine the chili powder, oregano, salt, and pepper and sprinkle 1 teaspoon of the mixture over one side of the steak; rub it in with your fingertips. Place the steak, seasoned side down, in a baking pan and rub the other side with the remaining teaspoon of seasonings. Broil the steak to a little bit rarer than your usual preferred doneness.

Transfer the hot steak to a cutting board and cut it into long strips about 1 1/2 to 2 inches wide, giving preference to the meat's natural divisions. Thinly slice each of the still-hot strips across the grain on a slight diagonal. Place the slices and any juice from the steak on a dinner plate, spreading them out in a single layer so that the steam escapes rapidly to prevent any further cooking. Let the slices cool for about 15 minutes, or until they are room temperature; then cover them with plastic wrap or aluminum foil and refrigerate for several hours, in which time the steak will reabsorb its juices. Take the tortillas out of the refrigerator at this time and let them come to room temperature.

To assemble the burritos, lay 1 tortilla on your work surface. Drizzle a squeeze or two of lime juice over one side and spread it around with your fingers. Divide the steak into 8 equal portions; arrange 1 portion in a line in a single layer at the bottom half of the circle. Top with 1 tablespoon of the scallions and then 2 tablespoons of the tomatoes. Fold the bottom edge of the tortilla over the filling to cover it; continue rolling to form an open-ended cylinder. Fold just one of the open ends up about ½ inch to keep the contents from dribbling out; wrap 1 aluminum foil rectangle around this folded area to secure it. Wrap the whole burrito snugly in a length of aluminum foil and crimp the ends shut. Repeat this procedure to make 8 wrapped burritos. Refrigerate until ready to use—for up to 1½ days.

To Cook

Preheat the oven to 450 degrees. Allow 2 burritos for each serving. Set the wrapped packages directly on the center oven rack. Bake for 10 minutes; then unwrap and serve with dollops of sour cream. Wrap the bottom half of the burrito in a paper towel or napkin and eat out of your hand.

Bayou Beef Buns

Makes 6; serves 4 to 6
Cooking Time: 5 minutes

1 ½ pounds ground beef
1 cup chopped onion
1 12-ounce bottle chili sauce
1 ½ tablespoons light brown
  sugar

½ teaspoon salt
½ teaspoon cayenne pepper
6 bulkie rolls or kaiser rolls or
  torpedo rolls

Heat the ground beef and onion together in a skillet over medium-high heat; break up the meat with a spoon and sauté until no more pink remains; drain off all the excess fat. Stir in the chili sauce, sugar, salt, and cayenne pepper. Bring to a boil and then cover, lower the heat, and simmer gently for 5 minutes. Remove the skillet from the heat; set the cover ajar to let the steam escape and allow the mixture to cool to room temperature.

Spoon the mixture into a lidded container, cover, and refrigerate until ready to use—for up to 3 days.

To Cook

For each roll, measure ½ cup of the meat mixture and 1 tablespoon of water into a small saucepan. Heat over medium-high heat, stirring for about 1 minute, or until boiling and heated through. Spread ½ cup of the filling over each split roll and serve.

Souvlakia

Serves 4
Cooking Time: 6 to 15 minutes

Pronounced "sue-vlah-key-ah," these Greek-style tacos are made with marinated and grilled cubes of lamb or beef. The hot cubes are wrapped in a softened pita bread and served with fresh vegetables and feta cheese in a tangy sauce

Half a leg of lamb (about 3 pounds), either the shank or sirloin half, or 2 pounds lean, 1¼-inch-thick beef, such as semi-boneless shell steak or London broil or beef kabob cubes
½ cup fresh lemon juice
¼ cup olive oil
¼ cup corn oil
2 large garlic cloves, smashed and finely minced
2 teaspoons onion powder
½ teaspoon pepper
½ cup plain yogurt
½ cup sour cream
1½ teaspoons snipped fresh dillweed, or ½ teaspoon dried dill

½ teaspoon salt
½ cup crumbled feta cheese (about 2 ounces)
¾ cup chopped ripe tomatoes
¾ cup peeled, seeded, and finely chopped cucumber
½ cup chopped onion, optional
4 Syrian-style pita breads, 7- to 8-inch diameter, preferably the thin, pliable kind from the supermarket deli section

4 10- to 12-inch-long skewers
Aluminum foil

Trim the excess fat from your choice of meat; if using lamb, cut big hunks off the bone; if using beef, remove the bone if there is one. Cut the meat into 1¼-inch cubes or chunks; count them as you put them in a medium-size mixing bowl; note the number on the bowl and set it aside.

Make the marinade by combining the lemon juice, olive and corn oils, garlic, onion powder, and pepper; blend until smooth. Pour the marinade over the meat and mix gently with your fingers; cover the surface of the meat directly with plastic wrap. Let the meat marinate for 1 to 3 hours at room temperature (use your own judgment on this if the temperature is over 80 degrees); then refrigerate overnight to complete the marinating. Refrigerate until ready to use—for up to 2 more days.

Make the sauce by stirring together the yogurt, sour cream, dill, and salt; then stir in first the feta cheese, then the tomatoes, and then the cucumbers. Cover with plastic wrap or aluminum foil and refrigerate until ready to use—for up to 2 days. Prepare the chopped onion, cover well, and refrigerate until ready to use.

To Cook an Individual Serving

Preheat the oven to broil, leaving the oven door slightly ajar; set the rack closest to the heat source. Thread one fourth of the meat cubes onto 1 skewer; place the skewer in a shallow baking pan.

Broil on the top rack, turning once at the halfway point. For either lamb or beef, cook for approximately 6 to 8 minutes for rare, 8 to 10 minutes for medium-rare, or 10 to 14 minutes for well-done. Slash one of the bigger pieces to test for the desired doneness.

During the last few minutes of broiling time, generously wet both sides of one pita bread with your hands. The bread should be almost, but not quite, dripping. While the meat is still broiling, put the bread on the very bottom oven rack of an electric oven or the very top rack of a gas oven (the setting will still be on broil). Heat for 2 minutes, or until the water evaporates and softens the bread; remove the bread before it can dry out or get crusty.

When the skewer of meat is done, place it on the bread, envelop it, taco-style, and slip the skewer out. Top the meat with ½ cup of the sauce and sprinkle on onion to taste. Keeping the pita folded shut, quickly wrap one side half in a length of aluminum foil to keep things from spilling out. Serve immediately, unwrapping the foil as you eat the souvlaki out of your hand.

To Cook Multiple Servings

Cook following the directions above, multiplying the portions accordingly.

Chicken Salad Burgers

Serves 4
Cooking Time: 10 minutes

1 large egg, lightly beaten
2 tablespoons strained fresh
    lemon juice
2 tablespoons mayonnaise
½ cup fine dry bread crumbs
½ cup scraped and finely
    chopped celery
2 5-ounce cans "Mixin'
    Chicken"

2 tablespoons butter
4 bulkie rolls or kaiser rolls or
    torpedo rolls, or 8 small
    hamburger buns
Mayonnaise and/or lemon
    juice, optional

In a mixing bowl, combine the egg, lemon juice, and mayonnaise; then stir in the bread crumbs and let them soak for 5 minutes. Stir in the celery. Drain and discard the broth from the cans of chicken and shred the meat. Blend the chicken into the mixture. Divide the mixture equally among 4 small custard cups, cover with plastic wrap or aluminum foil, and refrigerate until ready to use—for up to 2 days.

To Cook an Individual Serving

Melt ½ tablespoon of the butter in a small skillet over medium-high heat. Remove the meat mixture from 1 custard cup; shape it into a pattie that is the same shape and size as the roll you have—it should be about ¼ to ½ inch thick; if you are using 2 smaller rolls for each serving, make 2 patties out of the custard-cup mixture, each ¼ to ½ inch thick.

Sauté the pattie(s) for 2 to 3 minutes on each side, or until they are lightly browned; turn the pattie(s) over carefully with a spatula. Serve on split roll(s) with mayonnaise and/or lemon juice, if you wish.

To Cook Multiple Servings

If cooking more than 2 portions together, use just 1 teaspoon of butter for each portion and lower the heat if the butter browns too fast. Be careful when turning the patties over in a crowded pan.

Sausage Heros

Serves 4
Cooking Time: 5 minutes

1 ½ pounds Italian sausage,
   either sweet or hot
4 10- or 11-inch-long skinny
   hero rolls, or 8 small 5-inch-
   long hero or torpedo rolls

Your choice of filling, optional
   (recipes follow)

4 zip-lock sandwich bags

Bring a large pot of water to a boil. Prick both sides of each sausage at 1-inch intervals to let the fat escape and put the sausages in the boiling water. When the water returns to a boil, lower the heat and simmer for 30 minutes, uncovered. Remove the sausages from the water and allow them to cool on a plate; cover with plastic wrap or aluminum foil and refrigerate until cold. Slice the cold sausages on a slight diagonal into thin rounds. Divide the slices equally among the 4 plastic bags (there will be about 1 cup of slices per bag). Each bag will make 1 serving. Refrigerate the bags until ready to use—for up to 4 days.

To Cook an Individual Serving

Place 1 bag of sausage slices in a small skillet in a single layer and add 2 tablespoons of water; if you wish, add one portion of your choice of filling. Bring the ingredients to a boil over medium-high heat and boil for about 3 minutes, stirring now and then, until all the water has boiled off and the sausages begin to sizzle.

Spread the slices evenly in the split roll(s); cut the long skinny roll in half and serve.

To Cook Multiple Servings

Cook following the directions above, multiplying the portions accordingly and using a larger skillet. For each additional portion of sausages that you add after the first portion, add only 1 tablespoon of water.

Sausage and Onions

2 medium-size onions
3 tablespoons butter

4 zip-lock sandwich bags

Slice the onions into thin rings. Melt the butter in a skillet over medium heat. Add the onions and stir and sauté for about 10 minutes, or until they are limp but not brown or stringy. Allow to cool and then divide the 4 onion portions among the sandwich bags. Refrigerate until ready to use—for up to 4 days.

Sausage and Peppers

2 large sweet green peppers
1 large sweet red pepper
2 tablespoons butter

2 tablespoons olive oil

4 zip-lock sandwich bags

Seed all the peppers and cut them into thin strips. Heat the butter and oil in a skillet over medium heat. Add the peppers and stir and sauté for 10 to 15 minutes, or until they are soft but not brown. Allow to cool and then divide the portions among the 4 sandwich bags; refrigerate until ready to use—for up to 4 days.

Sausage with Onions and Peppers

1 medium-size onion
1 medium-size sweet green
  pepper
1 medium-size sweet red
  pepper

2 tablespoons butter
1½ tablespoons olive oil

4 zip-lock sandwich bags

Slice the onions into rings. Seed the peppers and cut them into thin strips. Heat the butter and oil in a skillet over medium heat; sauté the vegetables together for 10 to 15 minutes, or until they are soft but not brown. Allow to cool and then divide among the 4 sandwich bags. Refrigerate until ready to use—for up to 4 days.

Ready-Made Ham and Cheese Buns

Makes 6; serves 4 to 6
Cooking Time: 15 minutes

These made-in-advance, individually-wrapped sandwiches wait in the refrigerator. All you need to do is bake them for 15 minutes.

6 bulkie rolls or kaiser rolls or   8 ounces Colby cheese
   torpedo rolls   8 ounces boiled ham
9 tablespoons mayonnaise

Split each roll and spread it open. Spread 1½ tablespoons of mayonnaise between both open halves of each roll. Shred the cheese, about 2 packed heaping cups, and sprinkle equal amounts over all the 12 halves. Cut the ham into thin, julienne matchsticks; separate the pieces with your fingertips. Spread equal amounts of ham onto what will be the bottom half of each roll; close the rolls up.

Wrap each roll individually and quite snugly in a generous length of aluminum foil; make sure the ends are well sealed. Label and refrigerate until ready to use—for up to 3 days.

To Cook

Preheat the oven to 450 degrees. Allow 1 to 2 buns for each serving depending on appetites. Set the wrapped buns directly on the oven rack. Bake for 15 minutes, unwrap gingerly, and serve.

Grilled Cheese Tortillas

Serves 4
Cooking Time: 3 minutes

Easy enough for a child to make, these hot, half-moon tortillas are filled with cheese and Mexican-style flavorings.

16 ounces Monterey Jack
  cheese, shredded
4 tablespoons all-purpose flour
2 teaspoons chili powder
½ teaspoon cayenne pepper

4 tablespoons finely chopped
  scallions
4 teaspoons butter
8 8-inch-diameter flour tortillas

Combine the shredded cheese with the flour, chili powder, and cayenne pepper and mix with your fingers to coat all the shreds; then mix in the scallions. Package the mixture in either a covered bowl or among 4 zip-lock sandwich bags. Refrigerate until ready to use—for up to 4 days.

To Cook

Heat ½ teaspoon of the butter in a 10-inch skillet over medium-high heat; spread the butter evenly over the bottom. When the pan is hot, add 1 tortilla; sprinkle ½ cup of the cheese on top of the tortilla leaving a ½-inch margin all around. After about a minute, when the cheese is halfway melted, fold the tortilla in half and continue to heat for about half a minute more. Turn the tortilla over and continue cooking until the cheese is completely melted and the tortilla has golden brown spots on both sides. Allow 2 of these prepared tortillas for each serving. Eat out of your hand.

Skewered Mozzarella Loaves

Serves 4
Cooking Time: 15 minutes

Many layers of oozy, hot mozzarella between slices of crusty Italian bread are served with a dipping butter sauce of either anchovy-garlic or just plain garlic.

1 1-pound loaf thin Italian or French bread, about 4 inches wide and 20 inches long	Salt and pepper to taste
	1 2-ounce can anchovy fillets, optional
1¼ to 1½ pounds presliced mozzarella, 4 by 6 inches	2 garlic cloves, smashed and finely minced
8 tablespoons (1 stick) butter	
4 tablespoons olive oil	4 10-inch-long skewers

Cut the bread into equal quarters. Working with 1 quarter at a time, cut each straight across into ½- to ¾-inch slices. Cut the rectangles of mozzarella into thirds to fit the bread. Starting with the first quarter loaf, skewer the first piece of bread followed by a single third of a slice of mozzarella; continue the pattern ending with the last piece of bread in the quarter; set aside. Repeat skewering the other three-quarters in the same way. Use scissors to trim off the cheese that extends beyond the bread crusts; save the cheese for another use. Squeeze the contents of each skewer closer together so that all bread is flush with cheese.

Heat the butter and oil; brush a film of this mixture over a 10- by 15-inch (or similar) rimmed baking pan. Set the skewered loaves on this pan; brush the tops and sides generously with the butter mixture; also butter the exposed ends of the bread slices. Sprinkle the tops of the loaves with salt and pepper. Refrigerate the loaves, uncovered, for 10 minutes to solidify the butter; then cover and refrigerate until ready to use—for up to 3 days.

Pour the remaining butter-oil mixture into a blender, container. Open and drain the can of anchovies, add them to the blender, and then add the garlic. (If you don't like anchovies, omit them.) Whirl until puréed; pour into a small 1-cup jar; cover and refrigerate until needed.

To Cook an Individual Serving

Preheat the oven to 400 degrees. Allow 1 skewered quarter loaf for each serving. Use a spatula to lift the skewered loaf out of the pan; place it, upside-down, in a smaller ungreased baking pan. Bake for 10 minutes or until the cheese is melted and golden. In the meantime, stir and then measure 2 tablespoons of the anchovy and/or garlic butter; slowly heat in a small pan until melted.

Flip the loaf over and bake for another 5 minutes, or until it is golden and bubbly. Pour the butter into a small heatproof custard cup; set it on the dinner table. Remove the skewer from the loaf; cut the loaf lengthwise down the center. Eat plain or drizzle on or dip in the butter.

To Cook Multiple Servings

Multiply the skewer and butter sauce portions accordingly. Bake 3 upside-down skewered loaves on the original large baking sheet and transfer the remaining single skewered loaf to a different ungreased pan.

Steamed Corned Beef on Rye

Serves 4
Cooking Time: 6 minutes

2½ pounds flat cut raw corned
  beef brisket
8 slices caraway-seeded rye
  bread
Brown mustard to taste

Kosher dill pickle spears
Coleslaw (page 216)

4 zip-lock sandwich bags

Rinse the corned beef. To prevent the meat from curling, slash the fat that's on one side at ½-inch intervals, avoiding the meat. Bring a large heavy pot of water to a boil; add the corned beef, fat side up. Return the water to a boil; then lower the heat in gradual stages to maintain a gently bubbling simmer. Simmer, never boiling, uncovered, following the package directions, usually for about 3 hours. Replenish the water halfway during the cooking time.

Remove the cooked corned beef to a dinner plate to cool, uncovered; set the cooking water aside. When the corned beef is cool enough to handle, remove all the fat from the meat. Slice the meat across the grain on a slight diagonal into the thinnest possible slices (they should be no longer than the bread you will use). Divide the slices into 4 equal piles; put each pile into its own zip-lock bag; spread out the slices within like a hand of cards. Pour 1 tablespoon of the cooking water into each bag and seal airtight. Refrigerate until ready to use—up to 4 days.

To Cook an Individual Serving

Put 1 unwrapped portion of corned beef and 2 teaspoons of water in a small (3-cup) saucepan. Bring to a boil over medium-high heat, cover, lower the heat, and simmer for 5 minutes. If you wish to steam the bread slightly, add the 2 slices and cover the pan during the last half of the cooking time. Assemble the sandwich with plenty of mustard; serve it with pickle spears and coleslaw.

To Cook Multiple Servings

Cook following the directions above, using a 4-cup saucepan. For each additional portion of corned beef that you add to the first one in the pan, add only 1 teaspoon of water.

◈10◈

PORTABLE MEALS-ON-THE-GO

These hand-held, non-messy meals can go with you in the car, on the bus, or while you walk. They are all ready-made and take only 10 to 15 minutes to heat or bake.

Pizza Parlor Calzone

Quebec Tourtières

Fresh Bread and Sausage Swirls

Tidy Tacos

Beef and Cheddar Fillo Sticks

Turkey Piroshki in Sour Cream Pastry

Bundles from the Sea

Fondue Slices

Salami and Cheese Quiche Tarts

Other Portable Recipes from This Book

Pizza Parlor Calzone

Serves 4
Cooking Time: 13 minutes

1 1-pound loaf frozen bread
   dough
Olive oil
½ pound Italian sweet sausage
Several pinches of dried
   oregano, crushed

1 cup homemade or canned
   spaghetti sauce
4 to 6 ounces mozzarella
   cheese, shredded
All-purpose flour for dusting

Rub oil over all the sides of the frozen dough loaf; then wrap it in plastic wrap. Either let the dough thaw overnight in the refrigerator or let it thaw at room temperature until it is still slightly cold but not yet beginning to rise.

In the meantime, squeeze the sausage meat out of its casing; break it into small pieces and sauté it in a skillet over medium-high heat until no more pink remains; lower the heat to medium-low and simmer for 10 more minutes, stirring from time to time. Use a slotted spoon to transfer the meat to a dinner plate and allow it to cool. Discard all the fat. Stir the crushed oregano into the spaghetti sauce and set it aside. If you have shredded your own mozzarella rather than purchasing the preshredded kind, stir in a teaspoon of flour to prevent it from clumping; refrigerate until ready to use. Lightly oil a 12- by 15-inch baking sheet; set it aside.

Once thawed, cut the cold dough into 4 equal pieces; cover 3 with plastic wrap and set them aside. Lightly dust your work surface with flour. Hold the first piece of dough at arm's length in front of you; with your thumbs at the center, twirl the dough, pretending that it is a car's steering wheel and you are making a sharp right-hand turn. As you make the turn, work your thumbs closer out to the dough circle's edges. When you get to the edges, repeat twirling until you get a 6-inch circle. If the circle is irregular, let the dough rest over your fist and adjust it. Handle the dough slowly and gently: If you overwork it, the gluten will build up in the flour to a point where the dough will be too elastic to work with; if this does happen, let the dough rest, covered, for 10 minutes before using it again.

Put the 6-inch circle on your work surface; spread a tablespoon of the spaghetti sauce over the circle leaving a ¾-inch margin all around. Sprinkle 2 to 3 tablespoons of mozzarella over the circle of sauce. Distribute one fourth of the sausage meat, about ¼ cup, over just half of the circle. Drizzle 1 more tablespoon of sauce down the middle of the circle. Wet the dough margins with watered fingertips. Fold the non-meat side of the circle over the meat side to form a half-moon; crimp the edges shut. Transfer the calzone to the baking sheet; if you need to, use 2 oiled spatulas to make the transfer easier. Brush the calzone with oil. Repeat this procedure for the remaining dough pieces.

Brush one side of a length of plastic wrap with more oil; loosely cover the 4 calzone on the baking sheet with it. Let the calzone rise at room temperature for 1 to 2½ hours, or until they are puffed to a bit larger than your hand and some bubble-holes begin to surface. (If you wish, you can refrigerate the newly-covered calzone, instead, and let them rise at a later time for 1½ to 3 hours.)

Once the calzone have risen, bake them, uncovered, in a pre-heated 375-degree oven for 20 minutes. (If you wanted to eat them immediately, bake them 5 minutes longer.) Remove and let cool completely on wire racks. Cover with plastic wrap or aluminum foil and refrigerate until ready to use—for up to 3 days.

To Cook

Preheat the oven to 350 degrees. Allow 1 calzone for each serving. Place the uncovered calzone directly on the middle rack of your oven, with no pan or foil beneath. Bake for 13 minutes and serve.

Quebec Tourtières

Serves 4
Cooking Time: 10 minutes

Tourtières are little hand-held meat pies often found in Montreal. The tourtière recipe here has a potato pastry wrapped around a pork and onion, pepper, and spice filling.

2⅔ cups mashed potato flakes
  or the equivalent used to
  make 8 half-cup servings
1 cup all-purpose flour
1¾ teaspoons salt
1 large egg
3 tablespoons oil
About ½ cup water

¾ pound lean ground pork or
  1 pound not-so-lean ground
  pork, with no spices or
  flavorings
1½ cups chopped onion
½ teaspoon pepper
3 dashes of ground cloves
Oil for frying

Pour all but 2 tablespoons of the mashed potato flakes into a mixing bowl; reserve the remaining 2 tablespoons for later; blend in the flour and 1 teaspoon of salt. Lightly beat the egg in a measuring cup; add the 3 tablespoons of oil plus enough cold water to measure 1 cup, not counting the froth. Drizzle the liquid into the dry ingredients and toss lightly with 2 forks until there are many wet lumps; then form the mixture into a coarse ball of dough. Knead the dough for 5 to 7 minutes even though it won't look very smooth for your efforts; cover with plastic wrap and let it rest for at least 15 minutes while you make the filling.

In a large skillet, sauté the pork and onion together over medium-high heat, breaking up the meat and stirring, for about 10 minutes until no more pink remains. If there's excess fat, drain it off. Stir in the remaining ¾ teaspoon of salt, the pepper, and cloves; sprinkle on the 2 tablespoons of reserved potato flakes and stir to dissolve them. Then remove the skillet from the heat and allow the mixture to cool.

Pour enough oil into a heavy medium-size skillet to reach a depth of ¾ to 1 inch. Set the skillet over low heat for the time being. Cut the rested dough into 32 equal pieces; cover them loosely with plastic wrap. To make the first 2 pies, roll the first 4 dough pieces into balls and flatten them each into 4-inch circles, using either your hands or a small glass tumbler; don't roll the dough so thinly that it is unmanageable. Increase the heat under the skillet with the oil to medium-high. Put 1 heaping tablespoon of filling on 2 of the dough circles and flatten the filling slightly. Top each with a plain dough circle. Press the edges to seal; then secure by turning up the bottom dough edge and crimping it all around to form a little pie. When the oil is hot enough to sizzle a drop of flicked-in water, fry the 2 pies on one side until the edges begin to brown; then use a slotted spoon to turn them. When both sides are orangy-brown, transfer them to paper towels to drain. Continue to assemble and fry the pies, about 2 at a time, until all the ingredients are used.

Allow the pies to cool completely; then place them, without the paper towels, in a covered dish and refrigerate until ready to use—for up to 3 days.

To Cook

Preheat the oven to 350 degrees. Allow 4 pies for each serving; place them on a length of aluminum foil or an ungreased baking sheet and bake for 10 minutes.

Fresh Bread and Sausage Swirls

Serves 4
Cooking Time: 10 minutes

Oil
2 1-pound loaves frozen bread
   dough

1 ½ pounds Italian sausage,
   either sweet or hot

Rub oil over all the sides of the frozen loaves; wrap each separately in plastic wrap. Either let the loaves thaw overnight in the refrigerator or thaw for 1½ to 2 hours at room temperature, or until they are slightly cold but not yet beginning to rise.

Lightly grease a 13- by 16- or a 12- by 15-inch baking sheet with a film of oil; set aside. On a lightly floured surface, use your hands, pizza-parlor style, to pull the first thawed loaf into a 6- by 15-inch rectangle; place it on your work surface so that the shorter, 6-inch side, faces you. Squeeze the raw sausage meat out of the casings of half the sausage; break it into pieces; evenly spread and embed the meat into the rectangle of dough, leaving no margins. Starting at the shorter, 6-inch side, roll the dough up snugly, jelly roll fashion. Use your sharpest knife to cut the roll into 4 slices, each about 1½ inches wide; leave the end pieces just a little wider. Hold the first slice on the upturned palm of your left hand; cover with your right palm and gently turn your palms in opposite directions so that no sausage meat will escape; also, flatten the slice to about 1 inch thick. Put the slice on the greased sheet; repeat for the remaining slices. Cover the slices with plastic wrap while you follow the same procedure for the remaining dough loaf and sausage meat.

Loosely cover the sheet of slices with plastic wrap and let them rise for about 1 hour, or until doubled in size. (If you wish, you can refrigerate the newly-covered slices, instead, and let them rise at a later time for about 1½ hours.) Once risen, bake the slices in a preheated 400 degree oven for 20 minutes, or until lighly browned. Remove the sheet from the oven; loosen each bread swirl from the sheet with a spatula and allow to cool. Cover with plastic wrap or aluminum foil and refrigerate until ready to use—for up to 3 days.

To Cook

Preheat the oven to 350 degrees. Allow 2 bread swirls for each serving. Place swirls, uncovered, on an ungreased baking sheet or length of aluminum foil. Bake for 10 minutes and serve.

Tidy Tacos

Serves 4
Cooking Time: 10 minutes

Here are tacos-to-go that won't spill out of their shells

1 large egg
¼ cup bottled chili sauce
1 small onion, grated
1 small garlic clove, smashed
    and minced
2 teaspoons chili powder
¼ teaspoon ground cumin
¼ teaspoon salt

⅛ teaspoon cayenne pepper
¼ cup fine dry bread crumbs
6 ounces extra-sharp Cheddar
    cheese
1½ teaspoons all-purpose flour
¾ pound 80 percent lean
    ground beef
8 taco shells

In a mixing bowl, beat the egg lightly; then stir in the chili sauce, onion, garlic, spices, salt, cayenne pepper, and bread crumbs; allow to absorb for 10 minutes. In the meantime, cut the cheese into ¼-inch cubes (there will be about 1¼ cups); dust them with the flour, separating the cubes; set them aside.

Mix the meat into the crumb mixture; then use your hands to evenly mix in the cheese cubes. Divide this mixture into 8 equal portions. Press the first portion into an oval; slip it into a taco shell and gently press in place so that the meat is flush with the bottom; be careful not to crack the taco shell. Repeat for the rest of the meat portions and taco shells.

Put the filled taco shells on their sides on a broiler pan (or on a large rack or 2 cake racks placed over a rimmed baking pan). Bake in a preheated 350-degree oven for 20 minutes; then turn each taco over and continue baking for 20 minutes more. Remove from the oven and gently loosen each taco with a spatula so that the melted cheese doesn't stick it to the pan; allow to cool. Once cool, package the tacos, upright, in an 8- by 8-inch pan; cover with plastic wrap or aluminum foil and refrigerate until ready to use—for up to 3 days.

To Cook

Preheat the oven to 450 degrees. Allow 2 tacos for each serving. Put them on their sides in a baking pan. Bake for 10 minutes without turning and serve.

Beef and Cheddar Fillo Sticks

Serves 4
Cooking Time: 10 minutes

1 8-ounce box frozen Apollo Fillo, or half a 16-ounce box Athens Fillo Strudel Leaves	1 pound ground beef
	1 medium-size onion, grated
	Salt and pepper
4 ounces medium-sharp Cheddar cheese	6 tablespoons (¾ stick) butter
1 tablespoon all-purpose flour	6 tablespoons shortening

Allow the box of fillo to thaw in your refrigerator either overnight or for 8 hours; then let it stand at room temperature for at least 1½ hours before using. If you try to rush the thawing or attempt to work with cold fillo, it will only prove to be unmanageable.

Shred the cheese and then mix in the flour; measure to get 1 cup; set it aside. In a skillet over medium-high heat, sauté the beef and grated onion; when all the pink is gone, turn the heat to low and simmer for 5 minutes. Drain off all the excess fat and add salt and pepper to taste. While the meat is still hot, stir in the cheese until it has melted. Allow the mixture to cool to room temperature but don't refrigerate it.

In a small saucepan, heat the butter and shortening. Once melted, set the butter mixture over the lowest possible heat to keep it melted. Brush a 10- by 15-inch (or similar-size) rimmed baking sheet with a heavy film of the melted butter; set it aside.

To roll up the fillo sticks, have in front of you the fillo, the meat filling, and the melted butter. Spread the fillo out flat and cover it with a slightly dampened, non-terrycloth towel. (If you are using the 16-ounce box of 14- by 18-inch fillo, lay it flat and then cut it in half to get 2 rectangles that are 9 by 14 inches. Use the first rectangle plus a few more sheets from the second. Refreeze any remaining fillo.) Pick up 3 fillo sheets together and place them in a stack in front of you, short side facing you. Brush the top fillo sheet with the melted butter, leaving a 1-inch margin to the right and left. Spread one eighth of the meat filling, about ⅓ cup, in a line at the bottom, short side, leaving a 1-inch margin to the right and left. To make the first cylinder, roll up all 3 fillo sheets enough to cover the line of meat; tuck in the right and left sides all the way to the top of the sheet; brush the roll with butter and roll twice. Brush with butter and roll twice more. Brush with butter and finish rolling. Place the cylinder, buttered seam side down, on the baking pan; brush the top, sides, and ends with butter. Repeat this process 7 more times, working quickly so that the fillo won't dry out and crumble. When all 8 sticks are on the baking pan, brush them with all the remaining butter, making sure to cover the ends. Place the pan, uncovered, in the refrigerator for 20 minutes, or until the butter coating has solidified; then cover well with plastic wrap and refrigerate until ready to use—for up to 1½ days

To Cook

Preheat the oven to 475 degrees. Allow 2 fillo sticks for each serving. Use a spatula to transfer the fillo sticks to an ungreased baking pan. Bake for 10 minutes and then serve.

Turkey Piroshki in Sour Cream Pastry

Serves 4 to 6
Cooking Time: 12 minutes

3 ¼ cups all-purpose flour
1 teaspoon baking powder
½ teaspoon salt
11 tablespoons cold butter
1 cup finely chopped onion
8 ounces fresh mushrooms, finely chopped (about 2 ¼ cups)
1 teaspoon strained fresh lemon juice
3 tablespoons snipped fresh dillweed, or 1 tablespoon dried dill

1 pound raw ground turkey, fresh or frozen and thawed
1 large hard-boiled egg, finely chopped
Salt and pepper to taste
3 large eggs
3 tablespoons milk
1 cup sour cream

Combine the flour, baking powder, and ½ teaspoon of salt in a mixing bowl. Cut 8 tablespoons (1 stick) of the butter into bits; use a pastry blender to incorporate the butter into the dry ingredients until the mixture looks like coarse meal; cover with plastic wrap or aluminum foil and refrigerate.

Heat 2 tablespoons of the butter in a skillet over medium heat; add the onion and sauté, stirring, until it is limp; add the mushrooms and continue to stir and sauté until the mushrooms are soft and most of their juices have evaporated. Scrape the contents of the skillet into a medium-size mixing bowl; sprinkle with the lemon juice and stir in the dill; set it aside.

Heat the remaining 1 tablespoon of butter in the skillet over medium-high heat; add the ground turkey and sauté, stirring and separating, until cooked through. Scrape the turkey meat into the bowl with the mushrooms. Add the chopped hard-boiled egg and salt and pepper to taste. Stir the ingredients together with your fingers until they are evenly distributed; set the filling aside.

Preheat the oven to 400 degrees. Lightly grease 2 baking sheets and set them aside. In a small bowl, beat together 1 of the eggs and the milk; set the bowl aside. In another small bowl, beat together the remaining 2 eggs and the sour cream until smooth; pour the mixture into the chilled flour-butter mixture; use 2 forks to toss and combine. Form the mixture into a ball; knead it as quickly as possible on a lightly floured surface into a smooth dough. Cut it in half, wrap in plastic wrap, and refrigerate half. Working speedily, roll out the other half of the dough to a thinness of less than ⅛ inch. Use a 5-inch-diameter bowl or cookie cutter to cut out as many 5-inch circles as you can; don't be concerned if the dough begins to shrink of its own accord, but continue to work quickly. Brush the top of each circle with the beaten egg-milk mixture. Place about 2 rounded tablespoons of filling on one half of the first dough circle; form and slightly flatten the filling into an oval. Fold the other half of the circle over the filling and seal the half-circle edges by gently pressing with the tines of a fork. Place the pastry on the first baking sheet. Repeat this procedure to fill the first baking sheet with piroshki; brush their tops with more egg-milk mixture. Bake for 20 to 25 minutes, or until no more than just golden; allow to cool. Repeat for the remaining refrigerated dough, filling, and baking sheet. Transfer the baked piroshki to a lasagne-type pan; cover with plastic wrap or aluminum foil and refrigerate until ready to use—for up to 3 days.

To Cook

Preheat the oven to 350 degrees. Allow from 4 to 6 piroshki for each serving. Put them on an ungreased baking sheet or length of aluminum foil. Bake for 12 minutes, or until they are golden amber, and serve.

Bundles from the Sea

Serves 4
Cooking Time: 10 minutes

2 tablespoons butter
⅔ cup finely chopped scraped
    celery
12 ounces boneless cod fillets
2 lemons
Pepper to taste
1 6-ounce can crab meat
4 tablespoons mayonnaise
Dash of cayenne pepper

Salt to taste
2 8-ounce cylinders
    refrigerated crescent dinner
    rolls
1 large egg white
1 tablespoon water
⅛ teaspoon ground turmeric,
    optional

Melt 1 tablespoon of the butter in a saucepan over medium-high heat; add the celery and sauté for about 5 minutes, or until it is well softened but not brown. Cut the cod into, roughly, 1-inch pieces; stir them into the saucepan with the celery. Squeeze in the juice of 1 lemon and sprinkle with pepper to taste. Cover the saucepan and simmer over medium heat for 5 to 10 minutes, or until the fish is steamed so it is just flaky. Uncover and use a slotted spoon to transfer the fish and celery to a medium-size mixing bowl. Discard the cooking liquid. Allow the fish to cool then drain off any liquid at the bottom of the bowl.

Drain the crab meat well, squeezing out any excess liquid, and mix it into the cooled fish. Add 2 tablespoons of lemon juice from the remaining lemon, the mayonnaise, and cayenne pepper. Taste to see if you want to add any salt. Spread this filling on a flat dinner plate and set it aside.

Preheat the oven to 375 degrees. Lightly grease a 14- by 17-inch baking sheet with the remaining tablespoon of butter. Open the cylinders of crescent rolls and cut each sheet along the vertical and horizontal perforation lines into 8 rectangles whose shorter sides face you. Pinch the diagonal perforation lines on each side to seal the dough together. Beginning with the first rectangle, spread one eighth of the filling mixture (about ¼ cup) over the rectangle leaving a ½-inch margin. Starting at the short edge, roll up, jelly roll style, and pinch the 2 tips to seal. Set the bundle, seam side down, on the baking sheet. Repeat for all the rectangles.

Beat the egg white, water, and turmeric together; brush over each bundle on the baking sheet. Bake for 20 to 25 minutes, or until they are a rich golden brown. Loosen each bundle with a spatula and allow to cool to room temperature. Keeping the bundles in a single layer, cover with plastic wrap or aluminum foil and refrigerate until ready to use—for up to 2 days.

To Cook

Preheat the oven to 375 degrees. Allow 2 bundles for each serving. Put them on a length of aluminum foil or on an ungreased baking sheet. Bake for 10 minutes and serve.

Fondue Slices

Serves 4
Cooking Time: 15 minutes

1 1-pound loaf unsliced Italian bread	1 ½ tablespoons all-purpose flour
8 ounces sharp New York Cheddar cheese	2 garlic cloves
	1 cup dry red or white wine or beer

Cut the ends off the loaf; then cut the remaining loaf into 8 equal slices. Check to see that you can lay the slices snugly in either a 9- by 13- by 2-inch non-aluminum pan or in a slightly larger pan; remove the slices from the pan and set them aside.

Shred the cheese (you will get about 2¼ closely packed cups). Put the cheese in a bowl and stir in the flour to coat; set it aside. Halve the garlic cloves; rub the cut sides over the bottom of a medium-size saucepan. Pour in the wine or beer and heat over medium-high heat; then stir in handfuls of the cheese until it has melted smooth and is just beginning to bubble. Remove the pan from the heat and pour the hot sauce into the empty pan; spread it around evenly. Fit all the bread slices on top of the sauce and leave them there without turning. Cover the pan with aluminum foil and set it aside for 1 to 2 hours, or until the bread soaks up about half the sauce. Refrigerate the covered pan until ready to use—for up to 2 days.

To Cook

Preheat the oven to 425 degrees. Allow 2 slices of bread for each serving. Lift each slice out of the pan with the aid of a dinner knife or spatula and place it, sauce side up, on a length of aluminum foil or on an ungreased baking sheet; spread any remaining sauce from the empty spots in the pan back onto the bread. Bake for 15 minutes, or until bubbly at the center. Let cool, briefly, before serving.

Variation:

WELSH RAREBIT SLICES

Substitute 1 cup of milk for the wine and cook over medium-low heat. Add several generous dashes of cayenne pepper. Bake for 10 to 15 minutes, or until bubbly.

Salami and Cheese Quiche Tarts

Serves 4
Cooking Time: 10 minutes

¼ pound Genoa or hard salami or pepperoni, thinly sliced	¾ to 1 cup heavy or light cream
11 tablespoons cold butter	1 ¼ cups all-purpose flour
3 ounces Monterey Jack or Colby cheese	½ teaspoon salt
3 large eggs	4 aluminum foil pot-pie pans

Stack the salami slices and cut them in half. Stack the half-circles and cut the stack into thin matchsticks. Heat 1 tablespoon of the butter in a small skillet over medium-high heat; add the salami and sauté until it becomes limp and most of the fat has rendered out; don't let it get brown or hard. Put the salami but not the fat in a mixing bowl to cool. Shred the cheese to get a closely packed ¾ cup; add it to the salami.

Break 2 of the eggs into a measuring cup and beat lightly but not until frothy. Add enough cream to the eggs to measure 1 cup; mix this into the salami and cheese, cover with plastic wrap or aluminum foil, and refrigerate.

Preheat the oven to 450 degrees. Lightly spoon the flour into a mixing bowl; then stir in the salt. Break the last egg into a measuring cup and beat lightly. Add enough very cold water to measure to the 3-ounce mark, not counting the froth; set it aside. Cut the remaining butter into bits and use a pastry blender to quickly incorporate the butter into the flour mixture. Pour about ¼ cup of egg-water mixture into the flour mixture; toss with 2 forks, gradually adding more teaspoons of egg-water until the mixture wants to form a non-sticky dough. Working quickly, form the mixture into a coarse dough; then divide it into 4 equal pieces.

On a lightly floured surface, roll each piece of dough into an 8-inch circle; ease each circle into its pot pie pan; tuck the dough snugly under the rim of each pan so that it can't slide down during baking; don't flute or rest the dough on the rim. Prick each pastry with a fork. Bake for 10 to 12 minutes, or until the rims turn golden; remove and let cool to lukewarm. Lower the oven temperature to 375 degrees.

Gently break off the overlapping outside crusts from each baked tart so that the inside shell sides and rim remain. Fill the shells with equal amounts of the stirred-up salami-cheese filling. Bake for about 30 minutes, or until slightly puffed and a knife inserted at the center comes out clean. Let cool and then refrigerate until ready to use—for up to 3 days.

To Cook

Preheat the oven to 450 degrees. Bake the tarts for 10 minutes, or until warmed but not too hot to handle. Slide the tarts out of the pans; let them cool for half a minute; then eat them out of your hand.

OTHER PORTABLE RECIPES FROM THIS BOOK

Other portable, hand-held, non-sloppy meals from this book include:

❧ 11 ❧
QUICK ACCOMPANIMENTS &
READY-MADE SIDE DISHES

The preassembled side dishes here can be heated in less than 10 minutes. The made-in-advance salads simply await serving straight from the refrigerator. All are designed to complement the main dishes in this book.

Rice Pilaf

Ramen Noodles

Coleslaw

Spiral Pasta Salad

Potato Salad with Lemon and Parsley

Corn Salad

Honey-Lemon Carrot Salad

Tangy Cucumber Salad

Rice Pilaf

Serves 4
Cooking Time: 8 minutes

Here's a pilaf-on-hold especially designed to be 8 minutes away from completion. It isn't reheated so it's never mushy and it has the same sautéed butter-and-broth quality of its more time-consuming counterpart.

2 tablespoons butter
1 ¼ cups Uncle Ben's long-
   grain converted rice
¼ to ½ teaspoon salt

Pepper to taste
2 cups regular-strength canned
   chicken or beef broth

Melt the butter in a heavy saucepan over medium-high heat. When the butter sizzles, stir in the rice so that all the kernels are coated; add the salt and pepper. Constantly stir and sauté the rice so that it takes on a translucent quality. After a minute or two, the butter will begin to return to an audible sizzle and one or two kernels will begin to whiten. Losing no time, so that the kernels don't have time to pop, stir in the broth, bit by bit. Bring the broth to a full boil, cover, and lower the heat to somewhere between a gentle boil and a steady simmer. Simmer like this for 10 minutes only, or for 1 to 2 minutes more, or until the broth has been absorbed (disregard the rice package's cooking directions). Immediately spread the rice over 2 dinner plates to cool; this parboiled rice will not be entirely soft. Once cool, break up the rice and transfer it to a covered container. Refrigerate until ready to use—for up to 4 days.

To Cook an Individual Serving

Break up and measure 1 lightly packed cup of the rice into a small saucepan; add ¼ cup of water (or broth, if you wish). Cover the pan and bring to a boil over medium-high to high heat; once it boils, lower the heat to a steady simmer and simmer for 8 minutes. Turn off the heat and let sit, without removing the cover, for a minute or two to absorb any extra liquid.

To Cook Multiple Servings

Cook following the directions above, multiplying the portions accordingly.

Ramen Noodles

Serves 4
Cooking Time: 3 minutes

**3 3-ounce packages Oriental   2 tablespoons corn oil
noodle soup mix, any flavor**

Bring 3 or 4 quarts of water to a steady boil. Open the packages of Oriental noodles and set the 3 seasoning packets aside. Break each block of noodles into quarters; drop them into the boiling water and boil for only 2 minutes (even though the package directions will tell you 3 minutes), stirring the noodles frequently to separate them.

Pour the noodles into a colander and rinse with hot tap water to remove the excess starch. Toss the noodles and let them drain for 2 minutes. In the meantime, mix together the corn oil and the contents of the three seasoning packets to form a smooth mixture. Pour the still-warm, drained noodles into a medium-size bowl; drizzle the seasoned oil on top and use your fingers to coat all the noodles equally. Once the noodles feel cool, cover them with plastic wrap or aluminum foil and refrigerate until ready to use—for up to 3 days.

To Cook an Individual Serving

Set a small skillet with a non-stick surface over medium-high heat. Add ⅞ cup of the cold cooked ramen noodles and stir and sauté for a minute or two until heated through. Slide the noodles onto a dinner plate and serve.

To Cook Multiple Servings

Cook following the directions above, using a larger non-stick skillet and multiplying the portions accordingly.

Coleslaw

Serves 4 to 6
Cooking Time: None

1 medium-size head cabbage
1 cup mayonnaise
2 tablespoons prepared
  horseradish
2 teaspoons distilled white
  vinegar

1 teaspoon celery seed,
  crushed
1 teaspoon salt
1 teaspoon sugar

Shred the cabbage very thinly; then chop the shreds into 2-inch lengths. Put the cabbage into a large mixing bowl. Combine the remaining ingredients and stir the dressing into the shredded cabbage. Cover with plastic wrap or aluminum foil and refrigerate overnight to ripen. The coleslaw will keep for up to 3 more days in the refrigerator.

To Serve

Allow about 1 cup for each serving. Serve either chilled or at room temperature.

Spiral Pasta Salad

Serves 4 to 6
Cooking Time: None

1 12-ounce bag of three-flavor rotini primavera, or 4½ cups plain rotini (also called spirals or twists), or 1½ cups *each* tomato rotini, spinach rotini, and plain rotini
¾ cup mayonnaise
¼ cup bottled chili sauce
2½ tablespoons red wine vinegar
2 tablespoons strained fresh lemon juice
1 teaspoon salt
1 teaspoon sugar
⅛ teaspoon Tabasco sauce
¾ cup scraped and finely chopped celery
½ cup finely snipped fresh parsley leaves
¼ cup finely chopped red or sweet onion

Cook the spirals following the package directions until they are al dente; then drain in a colander and rinse under cold running water. Fill the spirals' cooking pot with cold water; return the spirals to the pot and let stand for a few minutes. Drain the spirals again and refill the pot with fresh cold water; return the spirals to the pot again so that they become cold and no starchiness clouds the water. Drain the spirals for at least 10 minutes in the colander.

Make the dressing by combining the remaining ingredients until well blended. Transfer the drained spirals to a bowl and pour on the dressing. Stir to coat the pasta with the dressing. Taste to see if you want to add more salt. Cover with plastic wrap or aluminum foil and refrigerate until ready to use—for up to 4 days.

To Serve

Allow 1 to 1½ cups of the salad for each serving. Serve either chilled or at room temperature.

Potato Salad with Lemon and Parsley

Serves 4
Cooking Time: None

4 to 5 medium-to-large
   potatoes, enough for 4
   servings
⅓ cup strained fresh lemon
   juice

¼ cup mayonnaise
1 teaspoon salt
½ cup finely snipped fresh
   parsley leaves
¼ cup finely chopped onion

Peel the potatoes and add them, whole, to a pot of rapidly boiling water. Boil, uncovered, for 20 minutes, or until they test done at the center. Drain off the cooking water and replace it with cold water to cover; let stand for 10 minutes. In the meantime, make the dressing by combining the lemon juice, mayonnaise, and salt in a bowl. Once blended, stir in the parsley and onion; set the dressing aside.

Drain the cooled potatoes and cut them into ¾-inch cubes. Put the potatoes into a medium-size bowl. Pour the dressing over the potatoes and stir to coat and separate any cubes that are stuck together. Cover with plastic wrap or aluminum foil and refrigerate until ready to use—for up to 3 days.

To Serve

Allow about 1 to 1½ cups of potato salad for each serving. Serve chilled or at room temperature.

Variation:

POTATO SALAD WITH LEMON AND DILL

Substitute 2 tablespoons of snipped fresh dillweed or 1½ teaspoons dried dill for the parsley and omit the onion.

Corn Salad

Serves 4
Cooking Time: None

2 10-ounce boxes frozen corn
kernels
½ cup mayonnaise
¼ cup sour cream
2 tablespoons strained fresh
lemon juice

½ teaspoon salt
¼ teaspoon Tabasco sauce
1 cup scraped and finely
chopped celery
⅓ cup finely chopped red or
sweet onion

Let the boxes of corn thaw to room temperature; then drain the corn in a colander. Do not cook the corn. In a medium-size mixing bowl, combine the mayonnaise, sour cream, lemon juice, salt, and Tabasco; once blended add the celery and onion. Pour in the drained corn and mix well. Cover with plastic wrap or aluminum foil and refrigerate until ready to use—for up to 2 days.

To Serve

Allow 1 scant cup for each serving. Stir the corn salad before serving chilled.

Honey-Lemon Carrot Salad

Serves 4
Cooking Time: None

About 1 pound carrots   4 teaspoons honey
¼ cup strained fresh lemon
  juice

Peel the carrots and shred through the shred side (not the grater side) of a cheese grater or use a food processor to get 3 lightly packed cups.

In a small bowl, blend the lemon juice and honey together until smooth. Stir this mixture into the carrots to coat them all. Cover the surface of the carrot salad directly with plastic wrap. Refrigerate until ready to use—for up to 3 days.

To Serve

Allow ½ cup chilled carrot salad for each serving.

Tangy Cucumber Salad

Serves 4
Cooking Time: None

3 large cucumbers
1 teaspoon salt
½ cup plain yogurt

¼ cup sour cream
Scant ⅛ teaspoon dried dill

Peel the cucumbers and remove the bitter tips. Cut each cucumber cylinder in half to get 6 cylinders. Up-end the first cylinder and cut the cucumber flesh from around the seed core to get 2 long, less-than-half-moon lengths and 2 thinner lengths; discard the seed cores. Repeat for all the cucumber cylinders. Slice the cucumber lengths on a diagonal into ¼- to ½-inch-thick slices to get about 4 cups of slices. Spread the slices in a single layer over 2 dinner plates. Sprinkle each dinner plate with ½ teaspoon of salt and stir to coat all the pieces. Let the cucumbers stand, uncovered, for 15 minutes.

Make the dressing by combining the remaining ingredients in a small bowl; set it aside. Use either your fingers or a slotted spoon to transfer the cucumbers to a medium-size bowl, leaving any excess liquid behind. Once in the bowl, drain off any liquid from the bottom. Stir in the dressing, cover with plastic wrap or aluminum foil, and refrigerate until ready to use—for up to 2 days.

To Serve

Allow 1 cup of the chilled cucumber salad for each serving. Once served, adjust the salt to taste.

❦ *INDEX* ❦